CWLA
Best
Practice
Guidelines

CHILD WELFARE LEAGUE OF AMERICA

WASHINGTON, DC

The Child Welfare League of America is the nation's oldest and largest membership-based child welfare organization. We are committed to engaging people everywhere in promoting the well-being of children, youth, and their families, and protecting every child from harm.

CHILD WELFARE LEAGUE OF AMERICA, INC.
HEADQUARTERS
440 First Street, NW, Third Floor, Washington, DC 20001-2085
E-mail: books@cwla.org

CURRENT PRINTING (last digit)
10 9 8 7 6 5 4 3 2 1

Cover and text design by Jennifer R. Geanakos
Edited by Julie Gwin

Printed in the United States of America

ISBN # 0–87868-895-1

Contents

CHAPTER 1

Introduction and Overview

The Child Welfare League of America (CWLA), in partnership with Casey Family Programs, developed these best practice guidelines to provide direction to child welfare agencies providing placement and child protective services (CPS). These guidelines provide agencies with an effective tool to develop administrative policies, procedures, and practices that will ensure a coordinated, effective response to reports of maltreatment of children in foster care.

CWLA is a national organization of nearly 1,100 child-serving agencies throughout North America. Both public and voluntary agency members serve children, youth, and families in need of pregnancy services; parenting skills; adoption, foster care, and kinship care services; mental health treatment; substance abuse treatment; child day care; housing services; independent living assistance; residential group care; juvenile justice services; and other essential supports. CWLA's mission is to engage people everywhere in promoting the well-being of children, youth, and families and to protect every child from harm.

The mission of Casey Family Programs' National Center for Resource Family Support is to develop and support a sufficient pool of competent families that can provide children and youth with safety, protection, stability, and permanency and meet their physical, emotional, cultural, and spiritual needs from infancy to adulthood to ensure they reach their full potential. Casey's National Center is a national clearinghouse and technical assistance center, providing agencies and families with a one-stop source of information, technical assistance, written materials, and referrals.

Many CWLA member agencies, foster parents, and kinship caregivers are responsible for providing safe, nurturing care for children in need of placement through family foster care services. The care children receive while they are the responsibility of the agency must meet their needs and be the highest quality for safety and nurturance.

Family foster care provides temporary care for children who, for safety reasons, cannot remain with their families. Foster care supports the family reunification process by providing safe and nurturing care for children while their families work to resolve the issues that led to the child's removal from home. When family reunification is not possible, family foster care provides an important bridge to new, permanent family relationships through adoption, guardianship, or placement with relatives who agree to provide permanent homes for their relative children.

The Need for Best Practice Guidelines

Child safety has long been a primary focus of child welfare. With the passage of the Adoption and Safe Families Act of 1997 (ASFA), the federal government underscored the importance of safety, permanence, and well-being in the delivery of all child welfare services, including family foster care.

It is most troubling when a report of suspected maltreatment is filed regarding a child who resides with a foster family. Reports of maltreatment of foster children occur for a variety of reasons. In situations in which maltreatment has occurred, it is crucial that the agency identifies the children at risk and protects them from further harm. Other reports may be unfounded, emerging from the complex dynamics of the foster care situation. This experience can be disruptive for children, their birthfamilies or legal families, and foster parents or other family members who may be the subject of the allegations. In each situation, it is important to document and ensure the safety of children while minimizing potential disruption and trauma that can be experienced by the child, foster family, and birthfamily.

Although public child protection agencies generally have well-developed strategies for investigating reports of maltreatment of children living in their own homes, less direction is provided for addressing maltreatment reports of children residing in foster care. Some states and agencies have well-developed policies and practices in this area, but others do not, and practices are inconsistent across jurisdictions. More guidance is needed to inform the process of investigating reports of maltreatment of foster children. CWLA's best practice guidelines are intended to provide such guidance.

These practice guidelines grew out of the need to go beyond current resources and respond to new developments in the field:

- The field needs consistent, quality practices in the investigation of out-of-home maltreatment. Currently, no uniform guidelines exist for such investigations, and practices vary across state agencies. These guidelines will provide agencies and workers with guidance that can minimize the distress and trauma often experienced by families and children.

- CWLA's *Standards of Excellence* for child welfare services, including family foster care, child protection, and kinship care services, speak broadly to best practice principles in child protection and foster care, however, they provide only general guidance to agencies regarding abuse and neglect in foster care. These practice guidelines speak specifically to these issues, promoting improved practice.

- In recognition that safety is a paramount consideration in all decisions affecting children in out-of-home care, the National Standards for Child and Family Services Reviews include the safety-related outcome of reducing the incidence of child abuse and neglect in foster care. These practice guidelines can serve as a resource tool to states in the development and revision of their investigation protocols and the training of CPS and foster care workers to better achieve this national outcome.

The Relationship Between CWLA *Standards of Excellence* and *Best Practice Guidelines*

CWLA's *Standards of Excellence* are goals for the continuing improvement of services for children and families. As goal standards, they reflect what the field collectively recognizes as the best ways to meet children's and families' needs. They provide a vision to which agencies and workers can aspire.

CWLA's *Best Practice Guidelines* elaborate on and operationalize practice standards by providing more specific, detailed guidance for agencies and practitioners. As with practice standards, guidelines are informed by experts and represent the best thinking of professionals across program areas. They are not intended to provide step-by-step instructions on, for example, how to conduct an investigation. Rather, these guidelines identify specific activities that should be undertaken and issues that should be addressed by child protection and child placement agencies when someone files a report regarding a child in foster care.

The Guidelines Development Process

Two key data-gathering activities were vital to the guidelines' development process (CWLA, 2002).

First, on October 4, 2001, CWLA contacted members of the National Association of State Foster Care Managers and asked them to submit materials relevant to development of practice guidelines on out-of-home maltreatment:

- state legislation and statutory provisions that address the response to and investigation of out-of-home maltreatment;

- state and local policies that guide the agency in its response to and investigation of out-of-home maltreatment;

- written protocols and agreements that guide practitioners regarding their roles and responsibilities in responding to and investigating out-of-home maltreatment; and

- model programs and initiatives that are relevant to the agencies' responses to and investigations of out-of-home maltreatment.

CWLA received materials from 24 states. These materials proved invaluable in identifying strong practices and have been incorporated into these guidelines. The materials also pointed out state-to-state inconsistencies and areas in which practice development is needed. These guidelines attempt to address those areas.

Second, CWLA (2001) held a meeting on November 16, 2001, to hear from experts in the field of child welfare and family foster care. Participants included individuals with a range of knowledge, skills, and perspectives: representatives of public and private child welfare agencies, foster parents, researchers, and representatives of advocacy organizations. The discussion informed and enriched these practice guidelines.

The Legal, Policy, and Practice Context

The Legal Framework

Legislation provides a foundation, context, and stimulus for the provision of child welfare services. Selected statutes—the Child Abuse Prevention and Treatment Act of 1974 (CAPTA), the Indian Child Welfare Act of 1978 (ICWA), the Multi-Ethnic Placement Act of 1994 (MEPA), the Personal Responsibility and Work Opportunities Reconciliation Act of 1996 (PRWORA), and ASFA—contain specific provisions that both affect responses to and investigation of allegations of maltreatment in family foster care.

CAPTA, most recently reauthorized in 1996 (P.L. 104-235), established specific reporting and response protocols for states to incorporate into their child protection statutes. Since its enactment, CAPTA has been amended several times to strike a balance between protecting children and preserving the rights and privacy of families (CWLA, 1999a).

ICWA provides procedural safeguards in matters pertaining to the custody and placement of American Indian children. Of particular relevance are the provisions that (a) give tribes exclusive jurisdiction over American Indian children living on reservations, (b) require that tribal jurisdiction over American Indian child custody proceedings be honored, (c) ensure that tribes and parents of American Indian children have the right to be notified and intervene in state court proceedings, and (d) specify the order of placement preferences for American Indian children in foster and adoptive families.

MEPA requires that any child placement agency receiving federal funds make diligent efforts to recruit a pool of foster and adoptive parents who are ethnically similar to the children the agency is trying to place. This means agencies must try to recruit and retain parents of color, particularly African Americans, American Indians, and Hispanics/Latinos.

PRWORA expresses a preference for placement of children with kin when it is safe to do so. It directs that states "shall consider giving preference to an adult relative over a non-related care giver when determining a placement for a child, provided that the relative care giver meets all relevant State child protection standards" (Title IV-E Foster Care and Adoption Assistance State Plan).

Legislators intended ASFA's provisions to help states achieve permanency for children in a timely manner. ASFA requires states to conduct a criminal record check on prospective foster or adoptive parents before they can be approved for placement of a child eligible for federal subsidies. With certain exceptions, ASFA also requires states to file for termination of parental rights (TPR) with the courts if the child has been in foster care for 15 of the most recent 22 months.

Safeguarding Children in Care: Key Issues in Policy and Practice

In many ways, responding to reports of maltreatment of children in foster care is no different than responding to reports of maltreatment of children living in any setting. The responsible child welfare agency must apply the same rigorous policies and practices for screening and investigating these reports and ensuring child safety. The following are important in all investigations:

- Making child safety the primary focus of the investigative process. Agencies must gather and analyze information so that they can make a sound determination of the current and future safety of the reported child and other children living in the foster home. They must ensure the safety of children in the home immediately to allow sufficient time to complete a comprehensive investigation. Child safety must remain the overriding concern at all stages of services delivery and in the management of all child welfare interventions.

- Preventing removal to avoid consequences of disruption and separation. Whenever it is possible to ensure the protection of children through the provision of supportive family services, agencies should minimize authoritative interventions.

- Making sound decisions regarding the determination to substantiate or not substantiate the maltreatment report.

- Making the provision of support to children, birthparents, and foster parents a key part of the investigative process.

- Using effective teamwork and clearly defined responsibilities to maximize the potential for good case outcomes and minimize the likelihood of additional trauma occurring as a result of an uncoordinated investigative process.

- Sharing decisionmaking based on input from multiple sources including the children, birthparents, foster parents, child welfare staff, and community professionals. This leads to responsive decisions and case plans.

- Respecting the rights of all parties involved in the investigation process, including foster parents. Respecting all parties leads to a less adversarial process and better case outcomes.

- Performing thorough documentation of all intakes, interviews, observations, contacts, factual information, and decisions. Documentation is a critical part of effective practice.

- Requiring notification of the child abuse registry and the licensing and regulatory entity at the conclusion of investigations, as warranted.

When a report of maltreatment is made in behalf of a foster child, additional issues and challenges must be addressed:

- Increased accountability and liability of the child welfare agency. Agencies must hold themselves and foster care providers to high standards of care when they accept responsibility for the care of a child who has been removed from his or her home.

- Possible multiple investigations conducted jointly or concurrently. Agencies must provide all parties involved with timely, relevant information, and must coordinate their activities to maximize information sharing and quality decisionmaking while minimizing disruption to the child, the birthparents, and the foster family.

- Multiple parties involved in an emotionally challenging experience. The process must be responsive to all of the parties involved— children, birthfamilies, foster families, and child welfare staff.

- The participation of foster parents as valued members of the professional child welfare team. Although the investigation must be thorough and agencies must take protective action when necessary to ensure children's safety, they must also treat foster parents with dignity and include them in the process to the greatest extent possible.

A Delicate Balancing Act

Investigating allegations of child maltreatment in foster homes is a delicate balancing act. Providing foster care can be highly stressful, leading some caregivers to become vulnerable to maltreating children in their care. Other factors can increase the risk that a report will be filed when no maltreatment has actually occurred. Factors that increase caregivers' vulnerability or stress and may increase the risk of maltreatment include:

- Caring for children with serious emotional needs and a history of maltreatment—either known or unknown—can be very challenging for any foster parent. Without adequate training on how to best meet the complicated needs of these children, caregivers may have limited understanding and skill and, consequently, may respond inappropriately to the child's difficult behavior.

- Even with training, not everyone can be well equipped to care for challenging children. Agencies must apply the highest screening standards in the selection and licensing processes to minimize the possibility of maltreatment of children in care.

- Due to a shortage of foster homes, agencies may ask foster parents to care for too many children, leading to overcrowding. Agencies may pay insufficient attention when placing a child with a family in which the child's needs are not compatible with the foster parents' capacities and resources are inadequate.

- Foster care caseworkers with high caseloads are less able to have frequent contact with foster caregivers, leaving the caregivers isolated and without the support, partnership, monitoring, and guidance they need to cope effectively with the child's challenging behaviors (McFadden & Ryan, 1991).

Factors that influence the reporting of maltreatment of children in out-of-home care include:

- Children in foster care may be very visible to people in the community who, in good faith, may misjudge a situation and make a report in situations where no maltreatment has occurred.

- Because people view children in foster care as an especially vulnerable group, reporters may be especially vigilant and prefer to err on the side of caution when making decisions on whether to report concerns of possible maltreatment of children in foster care.

- Agencies with responsibility for the care or custody of children in foster care may be more likely to file complaints on borderline situations out of concern for liability and the risk of negative public perception if they do not report.

- Young children with limited verbal skills may have difficulties distinguishing, to others, the caregivers who may have abused them. An effort to talk about past abuse may be interpreted as abuse that is occurring in the present with the current foster caregivers (Carbino, 1991).

Some children who have suffered maltreatment may file a false report. Characteristics of children in out-of-home care that increase self-reports include:

- Some children may want to return home and see filing a report of maltreatment in the foster home as a possible avenue for reunification (Carbino, 1991).

- Some children may be angry at disciplinary measures and, in retaliation, report maltreatment.

- Some children may misinterpret the caregiver's actions and antici-
pate a punishment for their behavior based on prior experience.

- Some children, due to past abuse, may feel threatened by or misinterpret well-intended or benign foster parent behavior. For example, a child who has been sexually abused may be very uncomfortable with normal expressions of affection or intimacy within
the foster family and may misinterpret these behaviors as threatening (CWLA, 1999a).

The fact that certain stressors may increase the risk of maltreatment in
foster care merits a strong protective response that accurately identifies situations in which children have been maltreated and need protection. The fact
that circumstances can increase the risk that a report may be filed when no
maltreatment has occurred requires agencies to conduct highly skilled and
thorough investigations in ways that make foster parents feel respected and
supported through the process. In many situations, the nature of the interac-
tion with the agency can make the difference between whether a competent,
much-needed foster parent will continue to foster or will withdraw from the
experience feeling hurt, frustrated, and disillusioned.

The Scope of the Practice Guidelines

These guidelines provide direction to child protection and placement agencies
responsible for the care of children in foster care and for responding to reports
of maltreatment of children in this setting.

Chapter 2 outlines effective agency practices in enhancing family foster
care and helping prevent the maltreatment of children in foster care:

- selecting and educating foster parents;

- identifying families that meet a child's unique needs;

- training child welfare staff;

- providing support and monitoring;

- preparing children, foster parents, and birthparents for the child's
placement; and

- providing continuous quality improvement.

Chapter 3 describes a safe and responsive approach to the intake process
when a report has been filed in behalf of a child in foster care:

- roles and responsibilities during the intake process;

- the importance of objectivity and confidentiality;

- key activities to be conducted during the intake process; and

- the importance of teamwork during the intake process.

Chapter 4 extends the discussion to the investigative process, emphasizing child safety, coordinated work with partners, and minimization of trauma of children, birth parents, and foster families:

- roles and responsibilities of the child welfare team;

- safety assessment and planning;

- methods for conducting interviews with key parties; and

- investigative decisionmaking.

Chapter 5 addresses a number of important decisions that the child welfare agency must make at the conclusion of the investigative process:

- selecting a course of action following a determination of substantiation;

- responding to concerns of maltreatment regarding the foster family's birth- or adoptive children;

- notifying key parties of the determinations; and

- supporting children through transitions including removal, replacement, or return of the child to the foster home following an investigation.

CHAPTER 2

Preventing Maltreatment in Family Foster Care

The prevention of child maltreatment, whether in birthfamilies, foster families, or other settings outside the home, must be a priority for child welfare agencies. The most effective way for agencies to prevent child maltreatment in foster care is to create an agencywide preventive approach, based on sound administration of foster care and child protection programs, quality supervision, effective training, and frequent contacts between workers and foster families. Guidance for managing and administering these programs is provided in CWLA's *Standards of Excellence for Family Foster Care Services* (CWLA, 1995), CWLA's *Standards of Excellence for Services for Abused or Neglected Children and Their Families* (CWLA, 1999a), CWLA's *Standards of Excellence for Kinship Care Services* (CWLA, 1999b), and CWLA's *Standards of Excellence for the Management and Governance of Child Welfare Agencies* (CWLA, 1996). This chapter addresses critical issues for child welfare agencies to consider when attempting to prevent maltreatment in foster care:

- Prevention of maltreatment in out-of-home care begins with the careful selection, preparation, and training of foster parents.

- Staff must be adequately trained to understand the complex stresses experienced by foster parents and be prepared to provide assistance and support to ease those stresses and enhance the foster family's ability to cope.

- Staff must pay careful attention to the preplacement assessment and matching of children with foster parents who have the skills and capacities to provide safe and nurturing care.

- Staffing patterns must allow for adequate levels of contact with and monitoring of foster parents and must make important support services available to them during times of need.

- Families and children must be adequately prepared for placement and included in the planning process to the highest degree possible.

- Staff must regularly visit children in care to attend to child well-being and provide an opportunity to address concerns about the placement.

- Staff must make regular contact with others in a position to observe and assess the child's ongoing safety and well-being, such as teachers, therapists, and child care providers, to ensure a comprehensive, ongoing assessment of the child's functioning.

- Agencies should be actively involved in continuous quality improvement to strengthen services provided to children and families and address gaps in services and areas of need.

Selection and Ongoing Assessment of Foster Parents

Selection Criteria

Efforts to prevent maltreatment by a foster parent begin with a careful, thorough selection process that includes assessment of a prospective foster family's history, dynamics, caregiving skills, and motivation to provide care. A thorough initial assessment process helps the agency make appropriate decisions regarding approval and licensing and also facilitates a more effective assessment of the match between an approved caregiver and the particular child's needs. Rycus and Hughes (1998) identified categories for assessment of a foster or kinship family's capacity to meet the needs of a child. These include characteristics that enable the family to manage the caregiving experience without experiencing severe family stress and characteristics necessary to meet the special needs and promote the healthy development of children in care.

Identifying these strengths in foster parents should be a central focus of the selection and assessment processes. These processes must also include the same careful identification of any areas of concern about a prospective foster parent's capacity to foster.

Assessments of prospective foster parents should include feedback from all major systems in which the family is involved. Although this may feel intrusive to the applicants, the child welfare agency's responsibility in making these selection decisions requires that it knows as much as possible about the family's history, actual experience, and proven skills and abilities, as seen by others in the community who are in a position to view them.

Maintaining High Standards

Despite placement pressures resulting from a shortage of foster homes and a dedicated effort to place more children with relatives or other kin, placement agencies must maintain high standards when selecting foster parents. This also applies to ongoing experience with the foster parent—if problems present themselves, the agency must address them.

Across the country, the declining number of foster parents and increasing number of children in care have caused general shortages of foster homes and shortages of homes for specific groups of children (McFadden & Ryan, 1991). A primary concern is that these shortages can lead to less-than-adequate screening and assessment of foster families and increase the likelihood of poor placement matches and the risk of maltreatment. Pressure to place children should not cause agencies to inadequately address concerns regarding caregiving skills or inadequacies in other areas of the home assessment that may lead to less-than-adequate caregiving and increase the risk of maltreatment. Despite the shortages, agencies should not license applicants who are inappropriate for fostering (CWLA, 1995).

Over the last decade, the number of children in formal foster care with a relative has increased. When, for the sake of their safety and well-being, children need to be placed outside their homes, the first option agencies should consider is the home of a relative or other member of the family's kinship network. Although children who can be safely placed with their kin have advantages, agencies must develop appropriate selection and assessment processes and standards for kin placements. Agencies must offer kin caregivers quality selection and assessment processes that will provide safe, stable, and nurturing homes for children placed with their kin.

Mutual Selection, Information, and Feedback

The selection process must be a mutual one. Although the child welfare agency has the final responsibility for selecting and licensing foster parents, it must also provide prospective foster parents with opportunities to actively participate in this process, through careful self-assessment of the strengths, motivations, and potentials that they bring to the fostering experience. The agency should encourage them to openly explore any concerns they have about their abilities to effectively manage the complex tasks of providing safe and nurturing care for children who are likely to have experienced difficult and traumatic life events. To assist prospective foster parents with this important self-assessment, the child welfare agency must provide

- information about the demands of meeting the needs of children who enter the foster care system, the types of difficult behaviors that these children may present, and the special health, mental health, or developmental needs that the foster parent must address;

- opportunities to explore how the fostering experience may affect the caregivers and their families and the supports and resources available to them to successfully manage those challenges; and

- consideration of the caregivers' strengths, motivations, expectations, and potentials, in light of the realities of fostering children in need.

Discussion with and feedback from agency staff, experienced foster parents, birthparents, youth in care, and alumni and other prospective foster parents can help prospective foster parents make these important self-assessments. Group selection and assessment programs play a vital role in this process. Agency staff and experienced foster parents should jointly facilitate these groups. Experienced foster parents and birthparents of children who have been in care can add a realistic perspective of the fostering experience that is invaluable to prospective foster parents. This perspective can provide feedback to improve the quality of the selection decision. Honest feedback provided in a clear and respectful manner is necessary and helpful to people who are considering becoming foster parents.

Foster Parent Preparation, Education, and Training

CWLA's *Standards of Excellence for Family Foster Care Services* (CWLA, 1995, p. 96) identify key competencies that agencies should address when providing preservice and inservice training programs to foster parents. The most important are described here.

Children in foster care typically demand high levels of care and present special challenges for their caregivers. As a result, foster parents must have clear, practical information to help them understand difficult behaviors and address special needs. Foster parents must have the understanding and tools they will need to meet those challenges. The following information is particularly important:

- The agency's expected standards of care in foster families.

- The desired roles that foster parents perform as members of the permanency planning team.

- The inherent tension between agency staff's desire to find a placement for a child and the foster parent's need to ensure that the placement will work for the family.

- Positive methods of behavior management that are most effective with children who may have been exposed to maltreatment, trauma, and separation from their families.

- Definitions and examples of behaviors and methods of discipline that are abusive, neglectful, or otherwise inappropriate.

- The difficult and traumatic experiences of many children in foster care and how these experiences affect their the development and behavior.

- Foster parents' personal styles of anger management.

- The development and implementation of household structures, patterns, and routines that increase the level of safety and comfort of all children living in the home.

- The resources available to provide support and assistance to foster families and children in care, such as respite care, crisis intervention, and concrete resources.

- The importance of advocacy within the child welfare agency. Foster parents need to feel empowered to ask for the services and supports necessary to provide safe and nurturing care, without fear of being judged. They also need to be able to set limits with workers on issues such as the number and types of children placed in their care. The agency should give them all available information about the child at the time of the placement request, and they should be allowed to decline a placement. Although these matters are the responsibility of the child welfare agency, it is still necessary for the foster parent to assert these limits as well.

- The role of investigation in providing safety for children in out-of-home care, as well as information on what to expect if an allegation is made, the decisions that may be made about safety and short- or long-term removal, the involvement of other children and family members, and the rights and responsibilities of foster parents during an investigation process.

Again, experienced foster parents can play a powerful role and should be full participants in these training programs. The realistic and practical information that experienced foster parents can share with their new colleagues is unique and invaluable.

Training programs can also be enriched by the participation of youth who have been in foster care and by their birthparents. Foster parents can greatly benefit from learning about the challenges of fostering and the effects of out-of-home care from children and families who have lived through it.

Joint training of foster parents and social workers together can ensure common understandings of the expectations and challenges of fostering, provide clarity about roles and functions, and provide the basis for effective partnerships as foster parents and child welfare staff work together in behalf of children in care.

Kin Caregiver Preparation, Education, and Support

Kin caregivers face special challenges in providing care for their relative children. Education programs should be tailored to the characteristics that make kinship care different from care provided by unrelated foster parents. The child welfare agency should offer and require orientation and education for all kinship caregivers at the point of initial contact and on a continuing basis. Topics should include, but not be limited to

- the effect of abuse and neglect on children;
- the shift in authority and responsibility between the birthparent and the kinship caregiver;
- the role of the kinship caregiver as a change agent in the family and as a role model for positive parenting;
- alcohol and other drug issues, including managing a relationship and having contact with a chemically dependent parent;
- HIV/AIDS;
- issues specific to kinship parenting, including the stress of full-time parenting for the second time, the dynamics involved in parenting young children as an older adult, and the special emo-

tional stresses inherent in family dynamics with the birthparent and other family members; and

- agency policies and procedures that affect kinship families.

Meeting a Child's Unique Needs

Placing a child with foster parents who have the knowledge, skills, capacities, and experience to meet his or her needs is a crucial aspect of an overall agency prevention plan. An important part of the process is to identify the child's needs and strengths that must be addressed through foster care. These include the child's

- age and gender;
- cultural, spiritual, religious, geographic, and community needs;
- history and the effect of past maltreatment;
- difficult or unsafe behaviors, including offending or self-injuring behavior;
- special health, mental health, or developmental needs;
- required level of supervision to ensure the safety of the child and others living in the home;
- ability to tolerate closeness in relationships; and
- comfort with relationships with other children.

Children should be placed with foster families that can meet the child's needs. As with the foster parent assessment and selection, the most effective matching process is one that emphasizes honest and comprehensive information sharing, inclusion of important people, and group decisionmaking. The agency should:

- Provide prospective foster parents with clear and thorough information regarding the unique needs of the child and the child's family.
- Encourage prospective foster parents to carefully assess the degree to which they can meet those needs.
- Involve children and birthparents to the greatest degree possible. Inclusion in the process can lead to a greater sense of control and cooperation as well as a greater sense of comfort by both child and birthparent.

- Validate concerns of foster parents, children, and birthparents. Although, in some cases, further discussion and appropriate supports can increase the confidence of all parties that the placement can be successful, workers should be careful not to "sell" participants while ignoring legitimate concerns.

- Record specific strengths and preferences of foster families in their family file.

Agencies should carefully attend to the following:

- The strict avoidance of overcrowding of foster homes, which increases the possibility of maltreatment or other negative incidents.

- The combination of children placed in a foster home. Caution should be taken when placing children or adolescents who may pose a risk to other more vulnerable children in the home.

- Children with extreme health or mental health needs that require high levels of care and supervision. Only the most experienced and well-trained foster parents can provide such care.

- The strict avoidance of placement with foster parents who have not developed the necessary competencies to care for children with complex needs. These situations can overwhelm foster parents and children and increase the risk of actual maltreatment, false allegations, and other negative outcomes for the child, the foster family, and other children in the home. Placements that cannot meet a child's needs or that subject a child to unnecessary stress greatly increase both the trauma for the child and the likelihood of placement disruption (Rycus & Hughes, 1998, p. 737).

Child Welfare Staff Training

Training Competencies

Training child welfare workers in the placement process is an essential aspect of the child welfare agency's efforts to prevent maltreatment in foster care. Workers should be trained so that they acquire the necessary values, knowledge, and skills to effectively perform their job responsibilities.

Agencies should identify core competencies that must be attained by all child welfare workers responsible for working with children in care, their families, and foster families, as well as specialized competencies for workers responsible for foster parent recruitment and selection, licensing, matching, and ongoing support activities.

Table 1 identifies core competencies that should be included in training for all child welfare workers who will be involved in the response to and investigation of maltreatment of children. It includes only those competencies that have special relevance to the prevention of maltreatment, based on the advice and feedback provided by panelists at an expert panel meeting held in November 2001 by CWLA (CWLA, 2001).

Table 2 identifies a number of specialized skills that should be addressed in training programs for staff who will be involved in foster parent recruitment and selection, licensing, matching, and ongoing support. CWLA also developed these competencies in response to the expertise provided by panelists at an expert panel meeting (CWLA, 2001).

Joint Training Approaches

Much can be gained from joint training. Foster parents and child welfare staff must work effectively together to

- make initial placement decisions,

- problem solve how to best meet the special needs of specific children in the home, and

- determine the types of supports for foster parents and children in care that are necessary to ensure a safe and nurturing placement experience.

Joint training ensures that foster parents and child welfare workers have a common understanding of these important issues and lays a foundation for partnership based on mutual understanding and respect. Experienced foster parents should play a role in the training process. Worker and foster parent training teams provide effective modeling of collaborative relationships, with each party bringing a unique perspective and competence to the training experience. Youth in care and their parents also can provide an important perspective.

Support and Monitoring

The more effectively the agency supports foster families and monitors high-stress situations, the more effective it will be at preventing maltreatment. Certain key practices are important.

Table 1: Core Competencies for Child Welfare Workers

Value	Knowledge	Skills
Teamwork	Understand importance and dynamics of collaboration and teaming Understand importance of involving birthparents, youth in care, and foster parents in assessment, service planning, and problem resolution	Serve as partner on collaborative child welfare team Involve birthparents and children in inclusive planning and problem resolution
Healing/easing effects of harm	Understand potential effect of placement on children and foster families	Help children confront and cope with trauma related to removal from birthfamilies Recognize unique needs of children in care Help caregivers develop effective strategies to address those needs
Safety	Understand risk and safety factors for children residing in foster care Understand risk of maltreatment by other children placed in foster homes	Conduct safety and risk assessments Help foster parents minimize risk of maltreatment by other children in home
Meet basic needs Healing/easing effects of harm Nurturing relationships	Understand challenges of caring for children who have been maltreated Know types of supports that can be effective in addressing stress in foster families	Recognize stress in foster families Establish supportive relationships with foster families Identify and provide resources that effectively diffuse stress
Optimal development Self-determination	Understand need for open communication with children in placement	Establish positive relationships and develop pattern of open communication with children in care
Nurturing relationships Permanence	Understand importance of parent/child visitation in maintaining continuity and culture and achieving permanence	Develop plan for visitation that ensures safety and helps children make progress toward permanency goal
Nurturing relationships Permanence Optimal development	Understand importance of strengths-based, child-centered, family-focused practice	Promote attainment of permanence through strengths-based, child-centered, family-focused services

Table 2: Specialized Skills for Family Foster Care Workers

ASSESSMENT AND PLACEMENT	PROVIDING SUPPORT	FOSTER PARENT DEVELOPMENT
Conduct an inclusive foster parent selection and assessment process that leads to mutual understanding of foster parent strengths and identifies concerns about inadequate caregiving	Form supportive relationships with foster families	Help foster parents develop caregiving strengths and effectively address any caregiving capacity concerns
Make sound decisions regarding licensing of foster families	Recognize signs that a foster parent may be under stress and mutually develop strategies to lower stress	Develop a plan for visitation with foster families based on their unique needs for support and monitoring
Make appropriate placements based on the foster family's capacity to meet the unique needs of a child	Identify and access supports that can be effective in addressing stress within foster families	Develop a corrective action plan to address any concerns regarding the standard of care being provided in a foster home

Valuing, Respecting, and Including Foster Families

Child welfare agencies must create an organizational climate in which respect for foster parents is incorporated and reinforced in all practices. All agency training should include a strong message of respect and appreciation for those who open their homes, their hearts, and their families to children in need. Agencies must pay special attention to the relationship and power difference between agency staff and foster parents to develop effective trust and professional partnership. All agency practices should include the input and participation of foster parents. Foster parents should have a central role in broader agency planning and decisionmaking processes and be involved in governance through memberships on advisory groups or boards of directors.

Accessible Workers

Although child welfare agencies may use differing staff designs, it is essential that a staff person be assigned to providing ongoing support to foster families. This person should advocate for foster families' needs within the agency. Ongoing support and problem solving regarding children in care should happen on a routine basis and should be increased during times of stress. Levels of contact should be based on the foster family's need for support and monitoring, rather than an arbitrary use of standards. CWLA's *Standards of Excellence for Family Foster Care Services* (CWLA, 1995) sets monthly in-home contacts as a minimum standard. More frequent contacts may be necessary during the early part of a placement or when stress levels are high and the need for more frequent monitoring exists. An after-hours response should be available so that foster parents have assistance during any time of crisis.

Concrete Supports

Placement agencies must provide a range of concrete supports to foster families. Respite care is an essential support that must be available to all foster families, particularly when stress levels are high. Agencies should make in-home crisis or stabilization services available to foster families struggling to effectively address difficult life events or the challenges involved in caring for a child with a high level of needs. At times, foster families need support due to other stresses including family problems, divorce, elder parents' health, and so forth. Support at the right time can help the family preserve the placement and ensure the safety of the child.

Support Groups

Foster parent support groups can provide an important source of support and information for foster parents. Foster care agencies should promote the development and maintenance of these groups and should support foster parent attendance. For example, ensuring that child care is available can increase the probability that foster parents will take advantage of this unique form of support.

Mentoring

Mentoring relationships with experienced foster parents can be extremely valuable to newer foster parents as they begin to face the challenges of fostering. The practical advice, understanding, and assistance offered by their experienced colleagues can help many foster parents make a successful transition. A number of agencies have found that a 24-hour support line staffed by experienced foster parents provides the needed assistance and encouragement necessary to avoid a placement disruption or unacceptable treatment of the child.

Empowerment

Advocacy and self-care are vital foster parent skills. Agencies should consistently encourage foster parents to be strong advocates for themselves and their families. Through training and contacts with child welfare staff, parents should identify their needs, express their concerns, and make decisions that are healthy for their families and children. Child welfare staff must be prepared to expect and value this kind of involvement.

Preparation for Foster Care Placement

Adequate preparation of children, birthparents, and foster parents can provide a foundation for placement that can improve the goodness of fit, ease the transition, and reduce the number of unanticipated problems that can lead to high stress, poor coping, and placement disruption. The agency should give the child, birthfamily, and foster family thorough information about the placement plans and an opportunity to fully discuss the placement with staff.

Preparing Children and Youth

Children and youth can be helped during the initial transition into foster care by providing them with information about

- the range of feelings, such as anger, depression, denial, loss, and confusion, that children and youth may experience when placed outside their families;

- the changes and challenges facing children and youth placed outside their homes;

- the roles and expectations of foster parents, agency workers, and birthparents in supporting their placement;

- information about the family they may be placed with, such as lifestyle, descriptions, and pictures;

- the process of case planning and permanency decisionmaking;

- the reasons for their placement, the issues that must be addressed for reunification to occur, and the services and supports that will be offered to them and their families to support the reunification process;

- the importance of communicating their feelings and needs to foster parents and agency workers; and

- effective ways to negotiate and resolve conflicts in foster care.

This information should be delivered within the context of an ongoing, supportive relationship with a worker who will be available to support the child through the placement process.

Whenever possible, the agency should provide the child with an opportunity to meet and visit the foster family prior to placement. This can provide a sense of familiarity that may ease the transition. Birthparents can play a vital role in helping children accept placement. Child welfare staff should work closely with birthparents to help them provide permission and encouragement for children to accept the foster care placement and work to make a positive transition.

Preparing Birthparents

Birthparents need the same type of information as that provided to children. Misunderstandings and undue anxiety can be avoided if the birthparents are able to understand their children's behavior as they transition into foster care. Birthparents are less likely to feel isolated and alienated from the process when the agency's workers have provided them with information about the foster family and included them in the matching process.

Most crucial is a trusting relationship between the birthparent and the child's service worker. When birthparents believe that they can express concerns and that those concerns will be addressed, they are more likely to voice concerns than act on them in ways that may undermine the placement, including potentially making false allegations of maltreatment.

When it is safely possible, many birthparents can be helped to be more supportive of the child's placement if they have communication with and develop a relationship with the foster parents. Birthparents who feel accepted and respected by foster parents, and who have a firsthand knowledge of the foster parents' concern for their child and competence as caregivers, are more likely to be accepting, if not supportive, of the child's placement in care. This is another special relationship that usually requires facilitation and care to address trust and power issues that may be threatening to either the birthparents or the foster parents.

Preparing Foster Parents

A quality preparation process provides foster parents with comprehensive information about the child, the child's behavior and special needs, and the child's birthfamily, enabling the foster parents to assess their ability to provide the necessary level of care for the child.

Foster parents need to be helped to protect themselves against false allegations. Knowledge of any history of previous false allegations made by the child or the child's birthparents is useful. Important information includes the type of allegations that were made and the types of situations that triggered the false allegation. For example, a child who has been sexually abused may be very uncomfortable with male caregivers, and related anxiety and confusion could trigger a false report. This knowledge would enable foster parents to respond by developing a caregiving plan in which the child was not left alone in the care of a male foster parent and by ensuring that primary caregiving activities would be performed by the female foster parent.

A birthparent who is experiencing a sense of isolation and lack of control may attempt to assert some control though a false allegation. This knowledge could lead the agency and foster parents to identify more ways to actively include the birthparent in the placement process.

Continuous Quality Improvement

Continuous quality improvement requires ongoing evaluation of the agency's out-of-home care system for children who have been abused or neglected, including:

- casework practices, such as case planning, documentation, monitoring, and decisionmaking practices for children in out-of-home care;
- the effectiveness of supervision of the casework practices;
- analysis of the agency's process for recruitment, selection, and training of prospective foster, kin, and adoptive parents;
- assessment of foster and kin care program resources, including staff training, education, and workload standards;
- analysis of information regarding incidents of maltreatment in out-of-home care to identify trends and agency strategies for preventing harm and attending to appropriate nurturance; and
- analysis of outcomes related to child well-being for children in out-of-home care.

Agencies should have the administrative capacity and infrastructure supports to gather data on

- the needs of abused and neglected children and their families and the agencies that serve them,
- the current capacity to meet those needs, and
- resources needed to fill the gap.

To track attainment of desired service outcomes, agencies should regularly collect

- incidence reports,
- input from foster parents,
- input from birthparents,
- age-appropriate input from foster youth, and
- evaluations of client satisfaction.

The agency should conduct periodic case reviews for children in foster care. Through this process, the agency should review the permanency plan of each child in out-of-home care to ensure the safety of the child in addition to the appropriateness of the current placement.

Summary

Although child welfare agencies must be well equipped to address maltreatment of children in foster care, they should pay equal attention to preventing maltreatment by providing sound management of foster care and child protection programs, quality supervision, effective training, and ongoing support of foster families.

Prevention begins with a careful foster parent selection and licensing process, ensuring that foster parents have the capacity to provide safe and nurturing care. Maintaining high standards when selecting caregivers is of utmost importance. Foster parent training programs should be built around key competencies necessary to accomplish these tasks and should be enriched by the participation of experienced foster parents. Agencies must apply the same selection and licensing processes to kin caregivers. Educational support programs for kinship caregivers must prepare them for the unique challenges of parenting a child within their kinship network.

Identifying families who are prepared to meet the unique needs of a particular child is a vital aspect of the placement process. The most effective foster family–foster child matching process is built on honest, comprehensive information sharing; inclusion of key parties; and group decisionmaking.

Child welfare staff should be trained in the competencies that are fundamental to performing their specialized job tasks. Joint training of workers and foster parents provides a unique opportunity to learn together and develop strong partnerships.

Supporting foster parents and monitoring their needs throughout the placement process can help prevent maltreatment or inadequate caregiving. Agencies must create organizational climates in which foster parents are respected and included. Accessible workers, concrete support groups, mentoring, and encouragement to advocate for themselves and their families are important ways to assist foster families.

Finally, child welfare agencies must have strong systems of continuous quality improvement by which they develop and track quality processes, service delivery, and outcomes for the children and families they serve.

CHAPTER 3

Receiving and Responding to the Report

The purpose of intake is to gather sufficient valid information to make a determination as to the most appropriate response to a report of suspected maltreatment. This chapter outlines the key activities, roles, and responsibilities of child welfare staff involved in the intake process and discusses the unique issues that arise when a report is filed about a child in foster care.

Key Activities During the Intake Process

Four primary activities comprise the intake process:

- receiving the report,
- screening the report,
- deciding on the type and urgency of the response, and
- notifying parties of intake decisions.

Receiving the Report

The first obligation of the agency receiving the report is to gather valid information to make informed decisions as to whether the child is being or has been abused or neglected, the level of harm to the child, and whether the child is currently safe or at risk of harm. The first responsibility of the intake worker is to seek information from the reporter to answer these questions.

Screening the Report

An important part of the screening process is to evaluate the credibility of the report and the validity of the information reported. At the outset, all reports should be presumed to be credible. Certain factors, however, may increase the possibility of malicious or erroneous reports. Some birthparents or relatives may have negative feelings about the placement that they may express through an erroneous report of maltreatment by the foster parents. Children in placement may also make allegations out of frustration, confusion, or anger, or in an effort to return to home. Nonetheless, the fact that a child or other reporter has made an erroneous report in the past should not hinder a full and cautious screening of subsequent reports. In child protective services, workers have good reason to err on the side of caution by conducting a respectful, careful investigation rather than screening out a report that may actually be legitimate.

Timely contacts with child welfare staff who know the child, the birthfamily, and the foster family can help make the important determination of whether a report is being made in good faith. Information sought should include:

- the nature of relationships between the child and foster family;
- any history of false allegations on the part of reporter;
- any information about the child's history that might help the screener evaluate the current report made by the child; and
- any information regarding major events in the life of the child, the birthfamily, or the foster home that might have triggered a report of maltreatment.

Contacts with knowledgeable child welfare staff should be made whether the child has been placed through the public child welfare agency, a tribal agency, or a private placement agency. These contacts have the dual role of providing information relevant to the screening decisions and informing the team members who will play important support roles during an investigation. These contacts must be made in a timely manner and should not delay the screening decision beyond agency timelines. Immediate action to ensure the safety of a child should not be delayed by efforts to make these contacts.

Making Decisions

When a report is filed in behalf of a child in family foster care, the intake process must distinguish between reports that

- do not indicate maltreatment or concerns about standards of care, and require no further services;
- do not indicate maltreatment or concerns about standards of care, but do identify the need for further services;
- do not indicate maltreatment but do raise concerns about standards of care and possible licensing violations; and
- warrant a formal CPS investigation.

These decisions should be made with the benefit of the best information available to the worker and with sound supervision and group decisionmaking.

No Maltreatment or Concerns About Standards of Care and No Further Services Required

When a report raises no valid concerns regarding maltreatment, standards of care, or the need for services, the report is screened out, documented, and no further action is taken.

No Maltreatment or Concerns About Standards of Care But Further Services Needed

Although a report may not indicate that maltreatment has occurred, and no concerns exist regarding the standards of care being provided in the foster home, it may still indicate the need for services or supports. In such cases, in addition to documenting the report, the intake staff should provide all information about the report, including the identity of the reporter, to the child welfare staff responsible for providing services to the child and birthfamily, as well as to staff responsible for providing support to the foster family.

Differential responses allow for more than one method of initial response to reports of child abuse or neglect. The use of differential responses allows agencies to provide services to some cases without a formal determination of abuse or neglect. Called *dual track, multiple track,* or *alternative response*, this approach recognizes the variety in the nature of reports and that one approach does not meet the needs of every case.

Despite the variability from state to state, differential responses sanction service interventions as an appropriate response to reports of child abuse and neglect when, if provided, they stabilize the family and enable the foster or birthparents to better care for the children (Schene, 2001). Although the majority of states do not have a formalized, flexible method for offering a variety of services based on the presenting circumstances, community-based services, such as family counseling, respite care, self-help support groups, and in-home aides, can be used effectively to address service needs whether they are part of an established differential response or not.

No Maltreatment But Concerns About Standards of Care and Possible Licensing Violations

Staff responsible for making screening decisions must be fully informed about how to distinguish situations that may not reach the statutory threshold of maltreatment, but do indicate licensing or certification violations.

- Each state or jurisdiction should have clear guidelines available and staff training to aid staff in identifying these situations.

- Staff should be provided with a clear, consistent process for notifying licensing or certification staff of these concerns in a timely manner.

- Notification processes should be clearly developed between the agencies or units responsible for the intake and investigation of these reports and those units responsible for investigating potential concerns about licensing violations.

- The intake worker must document the referral and its disposition.

Reports That Warrant a Formal CPS Investigation of Alleged Abuse or Neglect

When workers believe that the child may have been abused or neglected by a caregiver, the report is screened in to conduct the CPS investigation. This decision should be made using reliable decisionmaking tools and protocols and by applying the same standards that are relevant to all reports of child maltreatment.

States differ regarding the time frames in which the investigator should respond to a screened-in report of maltreatment in foster care. Decisionmaking regarding the need for an emergency response should be guided by straightforward agency policies and protocols. Immediate response is necessary when a report shows that a child may be in an unsafe situation and at risk of immediate harm. Children are considered safe when they are not in imminent danger and no safety interventions are needed (CWLA, 1999a, p. 37). Information to be considered when making this determination at the receipt of the report includes:

- the child's location;

- the child's age and developmental functioning;

- whether the child may be an American Indian child requiring the added protections of ICWA;

- whether the person suspected of being responsible for the alleged maltreatment has continued access to the child;

- the seriousness of the allegation and the extent of harm that has been or could have been caused by the alleged maltreatment; and

- the physical, emotional, and mental ability of the child's caregivers to ensure the child's safety prior to the initial contact by the agency.

When this analysis indicates that the child may be at risk, immediate face-to-face contact should be made with the child by a professional with the ability to put a safety plan in place (CWLA, 1999a, p. 38). This safety plan may include such actions as removing the child from the foster family or limiting access to the child by the person suspected of the alleged maltreatment.

In many cases, child protection and licensing or certification concerns will coexist. In these situations, the child protection agency or unit and the unit responsible for investigating licensing violations should have procedures in place to effectively conduct these related but distinct activities simultaneously.

The child protection agency must provide explicit information to responsible staff regarding when a report of maltreatment in family foster care warrants a report to the law enforcement agency. Each state has its own statutory language and policy guidance identifying those situations. Guidelines for determining the appropriate response in a particular state must be accessible and clear, and child protection agencies must provide workers with training to enable them to accurately identify situations in which law enforcement should be involved. In situations in which a report will be addressed by the child protection agency and the law enforcement agency, best practices recommend a joint investigative process in which roles and responsibilities are clearly delineated.

Finally, child welfare agencies need to have understandable policies for reporting and addressing critical incidents, including serious injuries or child deaths. Agencies should also have procedures and protocols for critical incident stress debriefing to help staff, children, birthfamilies, and foster families who may be exposed to these painful and often overwhelming situations. CWLA's *Standards of Excellence for Services for Abused or Neglected Children and Their Families* (CWLA, 1999a, pp.156–157) describe development of these procedures.

Notifications

Intake staff responsible for the screening decision should ensure that they notify parties who will play important roles during the investigative process of the screening decision. Table 3 describes the specific purposes of the contacts. As in all CPS investigations, the CPS investigators should contact other parties, such as schools, health care professionals, and other community service providers involved with the reported child or family, as warranted and legally permissible, during the investigation of a screened-in report.

Agencies should pay special attention to the process of notifying children's birth- and foster parents.

Table 3: Notifications by Responsible Intake Staff

Contact Person	Purpose of Contact
Child protective services (CPS) investigator	Provide with information gathered during screening as well as contact information of other parties who will be involved in investigation.
Law enforcement agency	Immediate notification when report meets statutory or policy guidelines for law enforcement involvement. Contact information with assigned CPS investigator should be shared for planning joint investigation.
Tribal social service agency	If the child is American Indian, notify tribe immediately, provide with all relevant information, and involve in all investigative processes.
Placement agency	Immediate notification to agency responsible for oversight of family foster home. Make plans to close the home to new placements during investigation. Inform of any plan to temporarily or permanently remove reported child or other children residing in home.
Child and family service worker	Immediate notification of report and screening decision. Inform of all allegations and any actions to protect the safety of reported child and other children in home.
Licensing/certification staff	Immediate notification of reports that merit investigation for licensing/certification concerns. Contact information with assigned CPS investigator should be shared for planning joint investigation.
Foster parents	Immediate notification of any report involving child in their care and the screening decision.
Birthparents	Notification of report, provide with contact information of investigator. Inform that they will be contacted by the investigator.
Mandated reporters	Notified of screening decision in accordance with state statutes or policies. Recontact by the CPS investigator during the investigative process.

Notification of Children's Birthparents

Because birthparents are likely to experience a range of emotions when they are concerned that their children may have been mistreated in an out-of-home setting, the notification may be best provided by the child's service worker, who has an ongoing relationship with the family. Workers should

- give parents an opportunity to express their emotions and concerns,
- assure them that the safety and well-being of their child is the first priority, and
- assure them the agency will conduct a thorough and unbiased investigation.

In situations in which children may need to be removed from the foster home, the birthparents should be made aware of the move and provided with information, as appropriate, about the new placement. A timely visit between the birthparents and child should be arranged. In considering placement options, the worker should assess whether kinship placement or reunification is appropriate and consistent with the child's permanent plan.

Notification of Foster Parents

Workers should provide foster parents with information regarding any report of a child in their care and of the disposition of that report. Prompt, forthright, respectful notification can create an environment of cooperation that facilitates a straightforward investigation process and an ongoing constructive working relationship with the foster caregivers. Workers should conduct all actions and interactions with sensitivity and respect for caregivers, so that they feel supported rather than "burned" by the process.

Depending on the nature of the allegations, especially if criminal charges are involved, information shared with foster parents must be limited to that which will not compromise the ability of CPS, licensing authorities, and law enforcement to complete effective investigations.

Roles and Responsibilities

CWLA's *Standards of Excellence for Services for Abused or Neglected Children and Their Families* (CWLA, 1999a) define the roles and responsibilities of the social worker, supervisor, and agency administrators in protective services.

Although states and jurisdictions may assign the responsibility for receiving reports of maltreatment of children in family foster care to different agencies or units, and staffing patterns may vary between agencies, the following parties play key roles and carry important responsibilities in the process.

Social Worker

A specially trained and experienced child protection staff person should be assigned to

- receive the report;
- seek information from reporter and other professionals regarding the alleged maltreatment and the behavioral, emotional, and physical conditions of the affected child, other children in the home, and foster parents;

- make decisions regarding the disposition of the report; and

- notify appropriate parties of the outcome of the screening decision.

Supervisor

The child protection supervisor plays an important role in this process, including:

- providing consultation, guidance, and supervision to the social worker;

- ensuring that the worker meets agency standards regarding timely and effective screening responses;

- providing linkages to agency administrators, other units within the agency, and relevant outside agencies; and

- discussing and approving all screening decisions.

Agency Administrator

The agency administrator plays an important role in this process by ensuring that

- well-trained, knowledgeable, experienced, and competent child protection personnel conduct the activities related to intake;

- workers consistently use reliable decisionmaking processes and tools;

- the agency monitors the quality of the intake process on an ongoing basis;

- communication across agency units and with other key agencies occurs in a timely and effective manner; and

- intake processes comply with statutory and policy mandates.

The Importance of Objectivity and Confidentiality

Along with being fully qualified for conducting this important child protection function, agency staff responsible for the investigation of reports of maltreatment in family foster care must be objective and especially sensitive to issues of confidentiality.

Objectivity

The objectivity of responsible staff is important when responding to reports of maltreatment of children living in any setting. Objectivity can be influenced by personal values and biases that result in subjective screening assessments and decisions. A lack of knowledge about cultural differences and community norms can compromise the worker's ability to remain objective.

Objectivity is essential when allegations of maltreatment are made in behalf of a child in family foster care. Child welfare staff involved in the case in any way can have their objectivity influenced by relationships with the child and birthfamily or with the foster family. Ongoing relationships with the child and birth- or foster family can alter a worker's perceptions and perhaps affect judgments. For example:

- Workers with connections to the child and birthfamily may feel especially protective toward the child or birthfamily, angry or blaming toward the foster parents, or blaming themselves. These and a wide array of other feelings may interfere with objectivity.

- Workers with ongoing relationships with foster parents may have difficulty believing that abuse could occur in that family setting. They may be so invested in maintaining a placement that their judgment about the safety and appropriateness of that placement could be affected.

Agencies can address this need for objectivity by assigning intake and investigation responsibilities to child protection staff with no case responsibility for the child, the birthfamily, or the foster family. This allows for an examination of the allegations by someone whose judgment will not be influenced by previous relationships or investments. Child welfare supervisors play an important role in helping all workers involved in the process be aware of and address any feelings or attitudes that may bias the process.

Confidentiality

The rights to confidentiality and privacy protections are fundamental tenets of child welfare practice. Confidentiality merits special concern during the process of intake and initial assessment of a report of maltreatment of a child in family foster care. The privacy interests of children and families are significant and should be protected from unauthorized disclosure of information.

Foster parents often have professional relationships with multiple staff members in the child welfare agency and have a great deal invested in their professional reputations with these colleagues. They deserve the right to have those relationships and their good names protected from unnecessary information sharing within the agency during the intake and investigation processes.

Information regarding the report should be shared only with those staff members necessary to ensure sound information gathering, appropriate determinations, and safe decisionmaking for the reported child and other children placed in the foster home. Foster parents have the same responsibility to maintain the confidentiality of children placed in their homes and those children's birthfamilies, even during this difficult process.

Teamwork Throughout the Process

The protection of children depends on the collective capacity of all involved to contribute to and support the ability of families—whether they be birth-, foster, or adoptive families—to meet the holistic needs of children. Individuals must be willing to communicate, cooperate, coordinate, and collaborate with one another to effectively respond to the safety and protection needs of children. Teamwork is essential throughout this complex and sensitive process. Multiple participants may need to be involved in the response to many of these reports, and they require clear communication, joint planning, and coordinated responses. The type and quality of communication in this initial process can set the stage for successful cooperative work as the process moves forward. Good child protection practice is dependent on good information.

Summary

When a report of maltreatment is filed in behalf of a child in foster care, the intake process must meet the same standards as in all maltreatment reports. Fully trained and experienced child protection professionals must conduct the key activities.

To ensure objectivity, the agency should assign these activities to child welfare staff with no ongoing case responsibility for the child, birthfamily, or foster family. Information should only be shared with people who have a need to know to help the agency make accurate, safe decisions. The reputations of foster parents should be respected and protected to the highest degree possible.

It is crucial to seek information from involved agency staff and outside professionals with knowledge of the child, foster family, and birthfamily. Information gathered from these sources can help intake staff assess the accuracy and validity of the report.

Decisions made during the intake process should have child safety as the main priority, be based on sound information from multiple sources, and be guided by strong supervision and group decisionmaking.

If reports of maltreatment are screened in for further investigation, the notification process serves to inform a group of professionals who must work together to conduct an effective and well-coordinated investigation. A quality intake process is the best assurance of determining the most appropriate response to a report of suspected maltreatment, whether the child resides in a foster family or a birthfamily.

CHAPTER 4

Investigative Process

When information received through the reporting and screening process suggests that a child in family foster care may have been maltreated, a report is screened in and assigned to a child protection investigator for a thorough investigation. The investigation must assess the child's present and future safety in the foster home and determine whether the child was maltreated. It is important for all parties that these investigations be completed as expeditiously as possible.

This chapter discusses key activities during the investigation, including, safety assessment and planning, conducting interviews, gathering and analyzing information from multiple sources, and making investigation decisions; and key roles and responsibilities of members of the child welfare team.

Key Activities During the Investigation

Child welfare workers conduct five key types of activities during the investigation:

- planning and safety assessment,
- coordinating activities of multiple agencies,
- conducting investigative interviews,
- gathering and analyzing information from multiple sources, and
- making investigation decisions.

Planning and Safety Assessment

The assessment of safety for the reported child and other children residing in the foster home is a core activity of the investigation. Children are considered safe when no immediate or impending threat of serious harm exists and when no safety plan is deemed necessary to ensure that they will not be harmed.

The first step of an investigation is to determine whether it is safe for the child to remain in the care of the foster family while the investigation proceeds. This decision is based on information obtained through the screening process, contacts with and observations of the reported child and caregivers, and interviews of other key informants as warranted.

In making this determination, it is important to distinguish among core elements of safety and risk:

- *Harm* refers to any physical or emotional injury to a child as a result of maltreatment. Different forms of maltreatment result in different forms and levels of harm.

- *Threat* of harm include conditions or actions within the family setting that represent the potential for injury or trauma to the child.

- *Severity* of harm involves a determination of the how seriously a child may be harmed based on the behaviors and conditions that exist within the child's living setting.

- *Immediacy* of the threat involves a determination of when the threat may present itself. Some threats are immediately present or imminent, whereas others may present themselves at some time in the future (Holden & Morton, 1999).

These concepts provide a foundation for understanding the different purposes of safety assessment and risk assessment during the investigation, as described in Table 4.

Workers should assess safety across the life of a child's involvement with the child protective agency. This is an essential aspect of each CPS investigation. Children should not be removed as a matter of course in each and every instance in which a report is made. Placements need not be disrupted if the child's safety is not in question. Formal safety assessment tools, separate from risk assessment tools, are essential to determining the child's safety and providing a foundation for safety planning.

In situations in which a child is determined to be unsafe, a safety plan must immediately be put in place that ensures the child's safety while the investigation proceeds. Workers must determine whether caregivers can protect the child from any existing danger or threat of harm. Workers should consider support services and other interventions focused on providing safety. When, despite these services and interventions, the child's safety cannot be ensured in the foster home, then removal of the child is essential. Rarely should the decision to remove a child be made by any single individual (Rycus & Hughes, 1998, pp. 733–734). Chapter 5 discusses conducting removals in ways that minimize trauma to the child.

Table 4: Key Distinctions Between Safety and Risk Assessments

SAFETY ASSESSMENT	RISK ASSESSMENT
Concerned with immediate or imminent threats of harm	Concerned with likelihood of any future maltreatment
Concerned with harm that reaches a severe threshold	Considers any type of maltreatment and severity (mild to severe) and includes child well-being
Informs immediate safety plan	Informs longer term case plan

SOURCE: Adapted from the National Resource Center on Child Maltreatment (2000).

Risk assessment evaluates a range of factors that may contribute to the likelihood of child maltreatment at any point in the future. It takes place once a child's safety has been assured and identifies family, child, environmental, and historical factors that may contribute to future risk and that workers must address to prevent a recurrence of maltreatment. Risk assessment should also consider protective factors in the environment that serve to reduce or resolve the risks of future maltreatment (National Resource Center on Child Maltreatment, 2000).

Coordinating Activities of Multiple Agencies

Investigations in foster care settings may occur simultaneously with investigations of potential licensing violations. In addition, law enforcement investigations of possible criminal violations may also be occurring. In those situations, it is essential that professionals coordinate their activities to avoid duplication of efforts, maximize information sharing, and minimize the disruption and potential trauma to the reported child, the foster parents, the birthparents, and others involved in the process. Agencies involved should develop protocols and interagency agreements that delineate their roles and responsibilities, as well as procedures for conducting joint investigations. Training for everyone involved in these investigations should emphasize collaboration, teamwork, and leadership to productively participate in, coordinate, and progress in this process.

Conducting Interviews

The investigation of reports of maltreatment of children in family foster care rely on the same methods of information gathering as all CPS investigations. Investigative interviews should be conducted with

- the reported child,
- other children residing in the foster home,

- the foster parents,
- the person who is suspected of the alleged maltreatment, and
- the child's birthparents.

Interviewing Reported Children

Child protection staff who conduct interviews with reported children should be competent in

- identification of physical and emotional indicators of abuse or neglect and skillful observation of those indicators during child interviews and observations;

- the approach, methods, and tools used in conducting investigative interviews with children of different ages about suspected maltreatment;

- effective communication skills with children of different ages;

- creating a safe environment for the investigation;

- questioning techniques designed to gather valid information from children at different ages and levels of development;

- understanding child suggestibility and how differences in cognitive and language development affect the way children communicate and relay information;

- working with health professionals to document injuries to children in a timely fashion and assess those injuries in the context of maltreatment;

- maximizing the child's comfort and minimizing trauma in identifying and observing physical injuries that might be a result of maltreatment; and

- using supervision and consultation to enhance the quality of case practice and case decisions.

Providing a Safe Environment

Providing a safe environment for the investigative interview is crucial to the interview process. Children are more likely to provide accurate information about their lives and the allegations of maltreatment when they feel safe to do so. This sense of safety has two important components. First, they must feel physically safe. Children who have been maltreated in a foster care setting may fear punishment or reprisals for reporting and sharing information with the investigator. They must believe that sharing information about their lives and the reported incident will not put them at risk of harm.

Second, they must feel emotionally safe. They must believe that sharing information will not cause further emotional distress in their lives. Many children who have been maltreated in a foster care setting value the relationships in the foster family and fear the disruption of those relationships that may occur if maltreatment is confirmed. This may be the case especially when the relationship in the foster family has been long-term, when children are living with relatives or other kin, or when there is a plan for permanency for the child in that foster home.

Creating a safe environment for the interview requires a number of actions and considerations. The investigator should consult with the reporter, child welfare staff involved with the child, the birthfamily, the foster family, and the child, if appropriate, to determine an interview location where the child may be most likely to feel and be safe. Some children will feel safe being interviewed in the foster home, whereas others may not. In that case, investigators should interview children in neutral settings outside the foster home.

When the safety assessment has determined that the child is safe in the foster home and the investigator is considering interviewing the child in that setting, it is important that the child has expressed comfort or preference for that setting and that the child has privacy during the interview.

When the initial safety assessment has raised concerns regarding the reported child's physical safety in the foster home, the interview must occur in another setting. If the child continues to reside in the foster home, the investigator should periodically observe the child and the interactions between the child and the foster family in the foster home setting.

Prior to conducting the interview with the child, the child protection investigator, working closely with other child welfare team members, should assist foster parents and birthparents in helping the child feel safe. When these individuals support the child's honest sharing of information and reassure the child of their concern and commitment, the child is much more likely to feel safe during the interview process.

Children feel safer when they are in the presence of someone they know and trust. The physical presence and emotional support of the child or family service worker or the child's therapist may enhance the child's sense of safety and security. If support people are included in the interview, a discussion must occur beforehand regarding the roles of the parties in the process. It must be made clear to the support person that no coaching of the child can occur. The presence of these participants must not detract from the validity of the information gained during the interview process.

Minimizing the Potential Trauma of Multiple Interviews

Because licensing, certification, and law enforcement investigations often occur simultaneously with child protection investigations, children in foster care may be unnecessarily exposed to the disruption, confusion, and trauma of repeated interviews with different parties. Multiagency agreements and protocols for joint interviews, information sharing, and decisionmaking can satisfy the mandates of each agency and reduce the burden and pain of repeated investigative interviews.

If the investigator cannot interview the child, it is critical that the investigator be actively involved in the process of planning the interview to ensure that information necessary for the purposes of the investigation is obtained. Many models have been developed in the context of joint child protective and law enforcement investigations (CWLA, 1999a, pp. 94–101; Office of Juvenile Justice and Delinquency Prevention, 2000; Sheppard & Zangrillo, 1996, p. 21; Tjaden & Anhalt, 1994).

More than three-quarters of states have statutes authorizing some type of multidisciplinary team, although their use varies considerably across states and localities (National Clearinghouse on Child Abuse and Neglect, 2000). Teams may address child protection, treatment, or permanency issues, and may be agency, hospital, or community based. Child advocacy centers, for example, are child-focused programs in which CPS, law enforcement, prosecution, mental and physical health, and victim advocacy groups conduct joint forensic interviews and make team decisions about the investigation, treatment, management, and prosecution of child abuse cases. States should consider ways to adapt effective models to situations in which child protection, law enforcement, and licensing investigations occur simultaneously.

Assessing the Information Gathered from Children

In interviewing children, it is critical to obtain information that will help determine whether the alleged maltreatment has in fact occurred by the alleged offender.

Standard child interview procedures mentioned provide a foundation for evaluating allegations in the context of a child's statements, and the investigator must approach the interview with objectivity and openness. Information the child or another reporter provides should be considered credible, and the child's interview should be designed to gather information from the child that will confirm or disconfirm the allegation of maltreatment.

Children in foster care may report maltreatment by their foster parents when no maltreatment has occurred for a variety of reasons. The worker should carefully examine information gathered during the child's interview in relation to the child's history of reporting, the child's level of cognitive and language development, the child's emotional and mental health status, and the dynamics of the child's placement. This information should be carefully cross-checked against other data gathered in the investigation.

When children knowingly make false claims of maltreatment, it is vitally important to work with the child and others involved in the child's life to understand what led to the false report. The child's allegation may identify important needs for supports or services that must be addressed in future case planning.

Interviews with Other Children in the Foster Home

When workers are concerned that a child may have been maltreated in a foster home, it is essential to evaluate the safety of all children living in that home, including the foster parents' birthchildren and adopted children. Thus, during the investigation, the worker should try to interview and observe all children in the foster home. These interviews have the dual purposes of gathering information to evaluate the allegations made in behalf of the reported child and of determining if other children residing in the home may have been maltreated or are at risk of maltreatment. When there are potential safety concerns, the workers should complete formal safety assessments for all children. Conducting these interviews involves cooperation and coordination between the investigative worker, the licensing or certification worker, the service workers for each child, the foster care worker, and the foster parents.

The investigative worker and foster care worker should meet with the foster parents to explain the need for interviews and seek their cooperation. Workers should encourage foster parents to express their concerns about the inclusion of their birthchildren and adoptive children in this safety assessment process. The workers must address their concerns, and assure them of the objectivity of the process and the measures that the workers will take during the interview to minimize discomfort to the children.

Workers should notify the birthparents of other children placed in the home of their child's inclusion in the interview process and seek their cooperation and consent. The workers should inform them of all efforts being taken to ensure the safety and well-being of their children.

Interviews with Foster Parents

Interviews with the foster parents have multiple purposes:

- To gather information and evidence regarding the allegation and the safety of the reported child and other children in the home. When one or both foster parents are alleged to have maltreated the child, the interview must meet all of the requirements of any interview of a person alleged to be responsible for the abuse or neglect.

- To assess foster parents' ability to provide safe care for the reported child and other children in the home while the investigation continues.

- To thoroughly explore the allegations and provide the foster parent with an opportunity to discuss the factors that may have led to the report of maltreatment.

Interviews with foster parents must be respectful and must value foster parents as members of the child welfare team. Workers must give foster parents comprehensive information about the rationale for and the manner in which the investigation will proceed. When licensing or law enforcement investigations will be conducted simultaneously, the workers should thoroughly explain these related but distinct processes. They should include foster parents in developing an investigation plan that minimizes disruption to their families while ensuring that the goals of each investigative process are met.

At the outset, the investigator should explain foster parents' rights. The investigator should provide these rights in writing and repeat them periodically, as relevant, throughout the investigation. At a minimum, these include the right to

- be notified of the investigation;

- hear the allegations, in a way that protects the integrity of the investigation;

- be interviewed and contribute to the investigation;

- seek representation, if they so desire;

- receive timely notification of the investigation determinations; and

- have access to appeals and fair hearings processes.

Although these rights may vary from state to state, foster parents should be aware of their rights and they should be fully respected.

When interviewing a foster parent who is not alleged to have maltreated the reported child, a primary focus of the interview is to assess the degree to which that foster parent is willing and able to take any necessary actions to ensure the safety of the reported child and other children living in the home. This may result in the person alleged to be responsible for the maltreatment being temporarily removed from the home while the investigation continues. This obviously can be a very difficult choice for the nonoffending foster parent when the person allegedly responsible may be a spouse, child, or other family member. It is also important to assess the foster parent's attitude and feelings toward the reported child to determine the nature and quality of the current relationship between the foster parent and the child.

The child welfare agency should identify someone in the investigative process whose primary role is to provide ongoing support to foster parents. Often, a foster care worker or licensing or certification worker who has an ongoing relationship with the foster parents can best fulfill this role. In such situations, the worker must be adept at providing support while remaining objective and must be able to make difficult decisions that may be counter to the foster parents' wishes. Other experienced foster parents may serve as a source of support and advocacy for foster parents going through this process.

Interviews with People Allegedly Responsible for the Abuse or Neglect

Interviews with foster parents or other foster family members alleged to be responsible for abuse or neglect must meet all the requirements of any standard child protection interview. The primary focus of the interview is to determine if maltreatment occurred and who was responsible for the maltreatment. It is essential that the investigator describe the rights of those alleged to be responsible for the abuse or neglect in the investigation and be objective and respectful in all interactions.

Joint interviews may be appropriate when certification or law enforcement investigations are occurring simultaneously. Workers should share information regarding the allegations in accordance with state policy, to the degree that these communications do not compromise the integrity of the investigation. When licensing or law enforcement investigations occur simultaneously, these different processes may be confusing to the foster parent. Explanations should be provided orally and in writing for future reference.

When the person alleged to have maltreated the reported child is a child in placement or a birth- or adopted child of the foster parents, the investigator should:

- Determine if the alleged maltreatment did occur and if the youth alleged to be the perpetrator was responsible for that maltreatment. Workers must ensure the safety of the reported child and other children living in the home and address any ongoing risk of harm presented by the offending youth.

- Determine whether the maltreatment could have been reasonably prevented. Were the foster parents aware of the risk presented by the offending youth? Did the foster parents provide reasonable levels of supervision and control? Did workers place the child appropriately in a foster care setting? Are the offending behaviors beyond what can be safely addressed in a foster care setting?

- Determine an appropriate treatment plan that will effectively address the offending behavior. The child's or adolescent's offending behavior should be fully evaluated. The worker should identify the child's or adolescent's treatment needs and develop an appropriate plan to ensure that he or she will not present a further risk to children living in the foster home or elsewhere and that ongoing treatment needs will be addressed.

The foster care or licensing worker with an ongoing relationship with the family should take a central role in helping the family cope with this crisis and locating necessary resources. The workers should provide foster parents with the necessary supports and information regarding how to best manage the situation.

Interviews with Birthparents

The interview with the birthparents of the reported child is an especially sensitive and important one. Although birthparents will not have uniform responses, they are likely to react with a range of emotions including fear, anger, distrust, anxiety, or self-blame. It is natural to have doubts, concerns, and a lack of trust about the child welfare agency. The worker must address these feelings through honest and thorough information sharing. Birthparents should

- be included in the investigation,
- have information and be involved in planning for the ongoing safety and placement needs of their children,
- be treated with sensitivity and understanding, and
- receive ongoing support.

Birthparents as Reporters

Interviews with birthparents who have filed reports of maltreatment present a difficult balancing act for the investigator. First, as in all investigations, the investigator must receive the information presented by the parent and objectively weigh the information against important standards of evidence. Some questions to be addressed include:

- How did the birthparent become aware of the alleged maltreatment?
- What indicators of maltreatment did the birthparent observe?
- What statements did the child make to the birthparent?

Second, the investigator must be aware that for various reasons, some birthparents may file false reports. The investigator should carefully assess the validity of the report, including factors such as

- any history of making false reports,
- the birthparent's relationship with the foster parents and the agency,
- the presence of disruptive case events that may cause a parent to react by filing a false report,
- the history of caregiving provided by the foster parent,
- the strength of the evidence of maltreatment, and
- other forms of corroborating evidence.

When evidence exists that a birthparent may have filed a false report, the investigator should seek to understand what led to the report. He or she should carefully document this in the case record so that the history of false allegations is available for future decisionmaking and the agency can address the causative factors. Workers should routinely seek consultation and supervision in such cases.

The Need for Support

Receiving information that one's child may have been maltreated can be a terribly upsetting experience for any parent, especially when that child has been removed from one's home and placed in a foster home. It is vitally important that birthparents receive support throughout this process. To some degree, a sensitive and respectful investigator can provide this support. Support should also be provided by the child and family service worker with an ongoing relationship with the birthparents. The worker and birthparents should agree on clear roles prior to the interview for any worker present during the interview.

Analyzing Information from Multiple Sources

As in any investigation, all information gathered in these interviews should be cross-checked against information gathered from other professionals with relevant knowledge about the child and family, including:

- the child and family service worker;

- the family foster care worker or licensing worker responsible for ongoing support and monitoring of the foster family;

- other professionals working with the child, foster family, or birthfamily, such as children's health professionals, tribal social services, school personnel, and mental health professionals; and

- agency records related to any substantiated and unsubstantiated reports regarding the foster parents.

Community professionals from outside the child welfare agency often have information about the reported child, the child's birthfamily, and the foster family that is vital to making accurate investigative decisions. Thus, it is important to contact relevant professionals during the investigation. The investigator should also invite foster parents to identify professionals and others who they feel can add helpful information that will inform accurate investigative decisions.

It is extremely important to protect the privacy, integrity, and professional reputation of foster parents as much as possible during these essential communications:

- Investigators should be clear that although allegations are being investigated, they have not been confirmed.

- When sharing information regarding the foster family, workers should share only what is necessary to gain information that is relevant to making investigation determinations.

- When the investigator is seeking information from professionals whose primary involvement is with the foster family, he or she should obtain verbal and written permission from the foster family to ensure informed consent for release of this information.

The Decisionmaking Process

The investigator is responsible for making a number of significant decisions including those that pertain to a finding regarding the allegation; the child's safety; the child's placement; and supports and services necessary for the child, foster family, or birthfamily during the investigation.

The decision to substantiate a report must be based on clearly defined, consistent criteria. Different states use different criteria. It is important that criteria across states are consistent and straightforward. Reliable assessment tools that guide decisionmaking and protocols that standardize best practices create the most appropriate responses. Due to the investigator's specialized training, objectivity, and lack of ongoing case responsibility, it is important that this critical determination is the primary responsibility of the investigator. In all decisionmaking, however, the investigator should solicit input, consultation, and supervision to inform and guide the process.

Roles and Responsibilities of the Child Welfare Team During an Investigation

During the investigation, the investigator must work closely with the child welfare team to conduct a well-coordinated, effective investigation. Key members of the team include the CPS investigator, family foster care worker, child and family service worker, tribal social services personnel, licensing or certification worker, CPS supervisor and agency administrators, law enforcement investigator, birth- and foster parents, and involved community professionals. Table 5 describes the key roles and responsibilities of these team members.

Recordkeeping

All aspects of the CPS investigation must be well documented, including interview notes, collateral contacts, dates and times of investigative activities,

Table 5: Key Roles and Responsibilities of Child Welfare Team During the Investigation

Team Member	Roles and Responsibilities
Child protective services (CPS) investigator	Assumes lead role in coordinating activities of different parties
	Gathers information from staff with ongoing relationships with foster family and reported child
	Conducts ongoing assessment of child safety
	Decides, with consultation, to substantiate report or not
	Works closely with child welfare worker responsible for child in placement to develop safety plan or remove child when child is unsafe
	May, in some circumstances, take a child into protective custody
Family foster care worker	Shares knowledge of foster parents and children in the home
	Provides case continuity with ongoing support to the foster parents
Child and family service worker with primary case responsibility	Provides key information about child, family, and ongoing experience in foster home that puts allegations in historical and ecological context
	Assists investigator in conducting investigation by performing supportive activities, such as scheduling appointments or transporting child to interview
	Provides support to reported child and birthfamily
	Works cooperatively with CPS to ensure safety of reported child and other children in the home, including developing safety plans and removing children when necessary
Licensing/certification worker	Works cooperatively with CPS investigator to conduct coordinated investigation
	Shares information and appropriate activities to avoid duplication of efforts
	Makes determinations regarding possible licensing violations
	Develops corrective action plan to address violations
CPS supervisor and agency administrator	Provides supervision and consultation
	Leads or facilitates group decisionmaking processes
	Monitors compliance with statutory, policy, and practice mandates
Law enforcement	Leads the investigation if there is a criminal violation
	Gathers physical evidence, conducts interviews, and takes protective custody of child if necessary
	Works cooperatively with CPS investigator to conduct coordinated investigation

Table 5: Continued

TEAM MEMBER	ROLES AND RESPONSIBILITIES
Community professional	Provides key information regarding allegations
	Provides direct support and services to child and family
	May assist in interviews as member of multidisciplinary team
Foster parent	Provides nurturing care and support to children during process
	Shares relevant information regarding child, foster family, and allegations
	Cooperates with all aspects of investigation
Birthparent	Provides information relevant to investigation
	Provides support to child
	Participates in decisions regarding placement alternatives

collaborative efforts, and justification for conclusions and decisions. It is critical that the agency's recordkeeping systems allow the tracking of referrals and dispositions both by foster home and by child victim. When checking for a history of prior referrals, both avenues must be checked.

Summary

Child welfare agencies should see the investigative process as a collaboration. Although the CPS investigator plays a central role, other members of the child welfare team assist in gathering information and providing support to children and families throughout this potentially difficult process. The primary purposes of the investigation are to ensure children's safety and make key determinations, but staff should make every effort to provide support and minimize potential trauma and disruption that children, birthfamilies, and foster parents may experience.

Agencies should ensure that staff are knowledgeable and consistent in the application of decisionmaking criteria. Although the CPS investigator should have primary responsibility for the substantiation decision, the decisionmaking process should be guided by reliable tools and protocols, input from multiple sources, and group decisions. Finally, the documentation of all investigative activities is crucial, and the agency must keep its records in ways that can be easily retrieved.

CHAPTER 5

Postinvestigation Response

When a worker substantiates a report, the child welfare team needs to make important placement decisions regarding the reported child and other children residing in the home:

- Are children in the home currently safe?

- Has the investigation successfully addressed all safety and risk factors?

- Are children connected by strong positive relationships to the foster family?

The team must make decisions as to the future status of the foster home:

- Should the foster home be closed? If not, what type of corrective plan is necessary to address ongoing risk factors?

- How can the team address systemic factors that may have contributed to the maltreatment to prevent further concerns about the care of children residing in the home?

Other concerns may exist and require attention when reports do not reach the statutory threshold to be considered maltreatment:

- Are there concerns about the foster parents' ability to provide an acceptable standard of care that should be addressed through the licensing or certification process?

- What type of corrective plan is necessary to address those concerns?

- Are there placement issues that the worker must address to avoid further reports of maltreatment?

Important activities include:

- timely notifications of key parties regarding the decision,

- returning children to the foster home who may have been temporarily removed during the investigation, and

- provision of follow-up and support to the child, the birthfamily, and the foster family.

Finally, although the investigation must focus primarily on child safety, all parties must be aware that the report of maltreatment and subsequent investigation can negatively affect children's stability, permanency, and well-being.

Each of the decisions and tasks is significant, and different members of the child welfare team will have unique roles in carrying them out. Clearly, this phase of the investigation is one in which teamwork continues to be essential.

This chapter will discuss

- decisions and tasks following a substantiated investigation,

- decisions and tasks following an unsubstantiated investigation,

- notification of key parties, and

- ways to support children through transitions in placement.

Decisions and Tasks Following a Substantiated Investigation

The first consideration following a determination of maltreatment is the safety of the child and other children living in the home. Safety assessment is an ongoing process that begins with the start of the investigation and continues as the worker gathers more extensive information regarding the allegations, the caregivers, and the child. With the conclusion of the investigation, in addition to safety, other long-term decisions regarding permanence must be made.

Foster care is meant to be a service that does more than keep children safe. Children need to be in settings where caregivers meet their developmental needs and provide them with nurturing and supportive adult relationships. Along with safety, those criteria must be met as well if children are to remain with the foster family following a substantiated investigation.

Under what conditions might a child be considered safe to remain with a foster family following a substantiated investigation?

- When the adult responsible for the maltreatment is no longer living in the home and will not have access to the children living in the foster home.

- When the foster parents can ensure that the behavior of a maltreating child who continues to reside in the home can be safely controlled within the home setting and that the level of supervision is adequate to ensure no unsupervised contact with other children.

- When the level of maltreatment was less serious and less harmful than indicated by statutory threshold and the person responsible has demonstrated the necessary emotional and behavioral control to ensure that it will not occur again.

- When formal risk assessment indicates that the risk of future maltreatment in the foster home is low.

- When the child has a strong attachment to the foster parents, feels comfortable and safe, and wants to remain in the foster home.

- When the relationship between the child and foster family has the goal of permanence (the child is in a preadoptive or kinship home) and all of the above conditions are met.

In short, a child should only remain in the home when it is clearly safe and in the child's best interest to do so.

This complex decision must be made through a group decisionmaking process that includes input from all members of the child welfare team, including the child and family service worker, family foster care worker, foster parent, child, child's family, and key supervisory and administrative staff. The decision must be based on a thorough knowledge of the foster family, the foster home setting, and the child.

When the above conditions are met and it is deemed to be safe and in the child's best interests to remain in the home:

- the agency should be responsible for closely monitoring and working with the foster parents to address any ongoing concerns or risk factors;

- the agency's contacts with the foster parents and the child should be increased and the situation carefully monitored; and

- the agency should help the foster family attain any outside supports and services, such as respite or health care, needed to address any concerns.

Decisions regarding the ongoing licensing of the foster home should be made based on the foster parents' ability to provide safe and nurturing care for the reported child and other children placed in the home. Options regarding the status of the foster home include:

- removing the reported child and other children placed there and permanently closing the home and terminating or revoking the license;

- preventing any additional placements with the family, with the worker ensuring that no new placements can be made by neighboring counties or agencies and that the agency itself has safeguards in place to ensure no other workers of the agency can place children there;

- helping the family successfully address any existing and ongoing concerns; or

- supporting the family in remaining an active placement resource.

Again, these decisions are not simple ones, and they can have great consequences for the child and family involved. Thus, they should be made with the benefit of sound group decisionmaking processes.

Finally, systemic factors can increase the stress on vulnerable foster parents and workers should consider these factors in the assessment, decisionmaking, and follow-up with foster families:

- Overcrowding of a foster home due to a demand that exceeds the supply of available foster homes for children in urgent need of placement.

- Placing children with challenging behaviors or high levels of need with foster parents who may not have the training and experience to successfully manage the behaviors and address the needs.

- Asking foster parents to accept the placement of a child with whom they do not feel comfortable.

- Providing inadequate contact with and resources and support to foster families, which can lead to their feeling isolated and overwhelmed. Such families may have less coping capacity than families receiving the supports and services they need to effectively take on the challenging task of caring for children with serious needs.

In such situations, the child welfare team should address these factors to prevent unnecessary stress for families providing care.

Decisions and Tasks Following an Unsubstantiated Investigation

Reports of maltreatment may be unsubstantiated for various reasons:

- The worker determines that an allegation was false.

- The reports were made by well-meaning people whose observations concerned them, but further investigation documented that no maltreatment occurred. In these types of situations, the safety of the children living in the home has been ensured.

- Concerns remain about the possibility of maltreatment or the level of care provided in the foster home, yet the worker finds insufficient evidence to substantiate the report, or the behaviors of concern do not reach the threshold of maltreatment.

Each of these situations involves unique challenges for the child welfare team.

False Allegations

False allegations may jeopardize a placement and traumatize the foster family. They can lead to damaged relationships and contribute to a foster family's decision to end their relationship with the agency. False allegations do occur, and when they do, they must be handled effectively by the child welfare team to avoid these negative consequences.

False allegations can be less disruptive when the agency educates foster families and the child welfare team about them in their training, intake procedures are effective at identifying them, and the team has conducted the investigation in an objective, respectful, and sensitive fashion. Workers should inform prospective foster parents of a child's history of making false allegations and the specific actions that parents can take to minimize the risk of recurrence.

Follow-up activities with the foster family, the child, and the birthfamily can effectively allay fears, repair relationships, and prevent future allegations. These objectives will be met when

- the foster parents and other family members have had the opportunity to discuss and resolve their feelings about the allegation;

- members of the team and the foster family understand the dynamics that led to the false allegation and have addressed those issues;

- the child or birthfamily has had an opportunity to discuss and resolve any negative feelings that led to the false allegation, and the team has discussed conflictual issues;

- the foster family and the placement agency have debriefed following this experience; and

- the foster parents have addressed any concerns about how the agency managed the experience.

When Concerns Remain

When the reported incident or behavior does not reach the level of maltreatment but raises concerns about the standard of care in the foster home, these concerns should be addressed by the placement agency or through the licensing or certification process:

- If concerns about licensing violations are present and an investigation of those violations has not commenced, the investigator should immediately share the concerns with designated licensing staff, the family, and the foster care worker who works directly with the foster family.

- The worker should clearly identify the issues and develop and monitor a corrective plan to address the issues.

- Decisions regarding continued placement should be based on an assessment that the child is safe and that the home effectively addresses the child's needs. When this is not the case, the worker should consider a different placement.

Concerns of Maltreatment Regarding the Foster Family's Birth- or Adoptive Children

When, during the course of the investigation, the investigator has reason to suspect that someone has maltreated birth- or adoptive children living in the foster home, people with direct information should file a report of maltreatment with the CPS agency and the agency should initiate an independent investigation.

Notifications

State statutes and policies identify those parties that should receive notice, and statutes provide time frames by which the notification of the investigative decision should occur. Notification of key parties of the investigation outcome should be done in accordance with these provisions. In investigating foster families, the following parties should be notified:

- child and family service workers with ongoing responsibility for the child and other children in the home;

- foster parents;

- family foster care and licensing workers;

- birth- or adoptive parents of the reported child and other children in the foster home;

- the reported child and other children in the home;

- the law enforcement agency, when a law enforcement investigation is ongoing or serious concerns exist that merit a referral to law enforcement;

- the tribal social service office, if the child or family is American Indian; and

- the mandated reporter.

Table 6 describes the purposes of those contacts.

Transitions in Placement of Children in Care

One of the most significant events that can occur during the investigation is the removal of a child from a foster home. Removal, whether temporary or permanent, may happen at the beginning of the investigation, any time during the investigation, or at the conclusion. When a change in the child's placement is necessary, workers should reassess the feasibility of reunification with the child's birthfamily, and if it is not a viable option, reassess other possibilities, including placement with kin, placement with a new foster family, or placement in a preadoptive home. Although agencies may be guided by specific policies regarding continued placement in foster care if maltreatment has been reported or substantiated, decisions regarding the removal of children should be based on how the decision will affect the child's safety, permanence, and well-being.

Removing the Child from the Foster Family

When a foster home is deemed to be unsafe or the child's needs cannot be effectively met in that home, then removal is a necessary and appropriate action. It is important to conduct the removal and new placement in a way that minimizes trauma:

- Provide children with clear information as to why removal from the foster family is necessary and give them an opportunity to discuss their feelings. A child's age and developmental status will affect how well a child can understand the removal issues, but in all cases, the worker should provide children with as much information as possible in ways that they can understand.

Table 6: Postinvestigation Notifications

CONTACT	ACTION	RATIONALE
Child/family service worker	Immediately notify through personal contact followed by formal written notification	Share all information to make accurate determination of safety and risk for children
Foster or preadoptive parents	Notify as soon as possible following the completion of the investigation	Provide opportunity to discuss decision, debrief, and explore implications of outcomes for their families and children placed in their home
Ongoing family foster care or licensing/certification worker	Immediately notify of investigation decision and all information necessary to help determine ongoing status of foster family and development of corrective plan	Provide support to foster family
Birth- or adoptive parents	Immediately notify of investigation decision Discuss decision to continue placement in foster home Provide ongoing support	Provide with opportunity to discuss maltreatment and concerns for their children Keep informed of ongoing efforts to ensure safety and well-being of their children Provide ongoing support
Reported child and other children in the home	Participate in joint meetings with key members of child welfare team.	Provide with information and support.
Law enforcement investigator	Immediately notify of investigation outcome and concerns as well as any actions taken to protect safety and well-being of children residing in home	Share all information relevant to law enforcement investigation and possible criminal violation
Mandated reporter	Notify according to state statutes and policies	Provide information regarding the decision, reason to accept or not accept the report, and the reason to substantiate or not substantiate if the report is accepted

- Whenever possible, provide children with the opportunity to meet with their foster parents and other children in the home to say goodbye and process the experience. Children need to be reassured that the foster parents are concerned for them and that the foster parents do not blame them or think they are bad. When there is an attachment between the child and foster parents, children may benefit from some form of ongoing contact with the foster family. Foster parents may be more able to offer this support even during this difficult time when they feel they have been treated respectfully and as vital to the removal process.

- When it is safely possible, provide a planned transition rather than an abrupt, unplanned removal. A deliberative transition can provide the child with more time to accept and adjust to the required changes.

- Provide children with support from the important people in their lives. The worker should try to provide opportunities for children to receive support, encouragement, and reassurance from their birthparents or kin.

- Ensure that the worker with whom the child has the strongest connection is involved in providing increased contact, information, and support to the child during this process of removal and new placement.

Placing a Child with a New Foster Family

When children are placed with another foster family following the removal, there must be careful preparation prior to and during the placement process. Providing straightforward information, encouraging discussion, processing feelings, and preparing the child for a new placement are vitally important activities that can help minimize the trauma of removal and placement.

Children should be helped to make a transitional connection with the foster parents prior to the move. Connection to a nurturing caregiver can make the move less frightening and overwhelming for the child. A brief period of visitation can allow these initial connections to occur. Younger children, especially, are more able to connect to one caregiver in the beginning. Efforts should be made to have the child first visit the foster home when the caregiver who will be the primary support is present, rather than have the child visit when the whole family is present, which can be a much more overwhelming experience. Once the initial engagement with the foster parent has occurred, the foster parent can then be the bridge for the child to meet the rest of the family (Rycus & Hughes, 1998).

When placing a child with a new foster family, short-term or longer term placement with appropriate kin can lessen the potential distress and disruption by providing familiar surroundings and supportive relationships for the child.

Returning the Child to the Foster Family

In some situations, children who have been removed from a foster family prior to or during the investigation will be returned when the investigation is completed. The decision to return the child to the foster family should be based on a sound assessment of safety and risk and a determination that this family best addresses the child's needs for safety, permanence, and well-being. When the worker has made this determination, the child will be prepared and supported during the transition.

The child, birthparents, and foster family should have opportunities to meet individually with the appropriate agency workers to discuss their feelings and concerns about returning to the foster home. The team should provide them with information regarding the findings and explore any issues. A joint meeting with the child and foster parents can help them process the events of the investigation and address ongoing concerns of either party. The worker should provide the child with information to assure him or her that he or she will be safe in the foster home. The foster parents should assure the child that he or she is welcomed, is accepted, and will not be blamed.

Breaking the ice and re-establishing comfort with each other following a difficult ordeal can be extremely helpful. Agency workers can help to facilitate this process.

If a child or parent has made unfounded allegations, the agency and foster parents should have a clear understanding of the issues that led to the allegations. The agency staff should work with all relevant parties to develop a plan to constructively address those issues. The agency worker must also offer foster parents an opportunity to discuss any concerns they have about the child's return to their home.

When a substantiated or unsubstantiated report identifies concerns regarding caregiving provided to the child, the agency must ensure that appropriate staff people work with the foster parents to develop a corrective plan that addresses those caregiving concerns. Responsible family foster care and licensing workers should carefully monitor the plan. All agency workers must be aware of the corrective plan and inform the monitoring staff person if any concerns arise during its implementation.

Finally, the child welfare agency should increase its level of monitoring and support. Both child and family service workers and family foster care workers should increase contact with the child and foster family during this transition, including more frequent phone contact, visits to the foster home, and other types of support as necessary. This increased contact should provide both support and careful monitoring of child safety and the stability of the placement.

Summary

At the conclusion of the investigation, the child welfare team should conduct a number of activities to ensure the child's safety, stabilize relationships, and minimize the trauma children may experience from placement transitions. The team must make important decisions regarding the ongoing status of the foster family as a placement resource for children.

Key principles employed throughout the intake and investigation process continue to shape decisionmaking and casework activities at its conclusion:

- The child's need for safety, permanence, and well-being guide all decisions and case activities.

- All members of the child welfare team have essential responsibilities during this process.

- Decisions of this magnitude must be based on sound information gathered from multiple sources through a disciplined and systematic process.

- Decisions should rarely be the responsibility of one person and should be shared by key members of the child welfare team.

- The agency should treat everyone involved in the process with respect and include them to the greatest degree possible.

- The agency should make all efforts to minimize the trauma and disruption that children, birthfamilies, and foster families experience during this process.

These principles are at the heart of the mission of child welfare, and they have served as the primary reference points for the development of these practice guidelines.

Glossary

Agency—An entity with an administrative structure, most often a government, child-placing, or regulatory entity.

Assessment—The process used with the family to determine if the child has been abused or neglected and if intervention is needed to ensure child safety and reduce the risk of future abuse or neglect. The process includes, but is not limited to, what has traditionally been called an investigation, and it occurs throughout the life of the agency's involvement with the family.

Best Practices—Recommended services, supports, interventions, policies, or procedures based on current validated research or expert consensus.

Case Plan—An agreement, usually written, developed between the family, the child welfare worker, and other service providers. It outlines the tasks necessary by all individuals to achieve the goals and objectives to sufficiently reduce the risk of future child abuse and neglect.

Certification—A credentialling process in which the agency demonstrates compliance with and maintenance of minimum standards and requirements as part of a non-governmental approval process.

Child Protective Services (CPS)—A process beginning with the assessment of reports of child abuse and neglect. If an agency determines that the child is at risk of abuse or neglect or has been abused or neglected, CPS includes the provision of services and supports to the child and his or her family by the public child protection agency and the community.

Collaboration—A process of individuals and organizations in a community working together toward a common purpose. All parties have a contribution to and a stake in the outcome.

Confidentiality—The protection of information obtained during a services intervention from release to organizations or individuals not entitled to it by law or policy.

Disruption—Unplanned discontinuation of a child's placement with a foster or adoptive family.

Family—Birthparents, adoptive parents, grandparents, siblings, foster parents, legal guardians, or any other person in a parental role.

Family Foster Care—Essential child welfare service for children and their parents who must live apart from each other for a temporary period of time because of physical abuse, sexual abuse, neglect, emotional maltreatment, or special circumstances. Children are placed in the homes of nurturing, licensed, trained caregivers.

Harm—An injury received as a result of physical abuse, sexual abuse, neglect, or emotional maltreatment.

Investigation—An inquiry or search by law enforcement or CPS to determine the validity of a report of child abuse or neglect and to determine if a crime has been committed.

Kinship Care—The full-time care of children by relatives, members of their tribes or clans, godparents, stepparents, or other adults who have a kinship bond with a child.

Kinship Foster Care—the daily parenting care of children by kin as a result of a determination by the court and the public CPS agency that a child must be separated from his or her parents because of abuse, neglect, dependency, abandonment, or special medical circumstances. In formal kinship care, the court places the child in the legal custody of the child welfare agency, and kin provide full-time care, protection, and nurturing.

Licensing—Compliance with and maintenance of minimum standards and requirements that are defined by law and amplified by rules and regulations. Such standards and requirements are aimed primarily at the protection of children and their parents but also offer protection to the agency in its assurance to the community that it meets these standards.

Multidisciplinary Team—A group established among agencies or individuals to promote collaboration and shared decisionmaking around the protection of children. Some multidisciplinary teams address issues related to individual children and families, whereas others focus more on communitywide prevention and protection strategies.

Out-of-Home Care—Array of services including family foster care, kinship care, and residential group care for children who have been placed in the custody of the state and who require living arrangements away from their birthparents.

Policies—Written requirements that direct business and service delivery practices of an agency. Policies should carry the approval of the agency's governing or advisory board.

Procedures—Written guidelines developed by an agency's administration to ensure that operational practices are consistent with board-approved policies.

Protocols—Interagency agreements that delineate joint roles and responsibilities by establishing criteria and procedures for working together on cases in which child safety or family well-being is of concern.

Respite Care—Temporary relief provided to caregivers to reduce stress, support family stability, prevent abuse and neglect, and minimize the need for a change in the child's placement.

Risk Assessment—An assessment of the likelihood that a child will be abused or neglected in the future.

Safety—A child is safe if an analysis of all available information leads to the conclusion that the child in his or her living arrangement is not in imminent danger of harm and no interventions are necessary to ensure the child's safety.

State Licensing or Regulatory Agency—The state body with statutory authority to license or regulate facilities.

Substantiated—A finding after the initial assessment that credible evidence exists to show that child abuse or neglect has occurred.

Unsubstantiated—A finding after the initial assessment that insufficient credible evidence exists to show that child abuse or neglect has occurred.

References

Carbino, R. (1991). Child abuse and neglect reports in foster care: The issue for foster families of "false" allegations. In M. Robin (Ed.), *Assessing child maltreatment reports* (pp. 233–248). Binghamton, NY: Haworth Press.

Child Welfare League of America. (1995). *Standards of excellence for family foster care services* (Rev. ed.). Washington, DC: Author.

Child Welfare League of America. (1996). *Standards of excellence for management and governance of child welfare agencies*. Washington, DC: Author.

Child Welfare League of America. (1999a). *Standards of excellence for abused or neglected children and their families* (Rev. ed.). Washington, DC: Author.

Child Welfare League of America. (1999b). *Standards of excellence for kinship care services*. Washington, DC: Author.

Child Welfare League of America. (2001). *State responses to allegations of maltreatment in out-of-home care: Summary of state analyses and key issues for consideration*. Available from http://www.cwla.org/programs/fostercare/statessummary.htm.

Child Welfare League of America. (2002). *NWG highlights—Child maltreatment in foster care: Understanding the data*. Washington, DC: CWLA National Working Group to Improve Child Welfare Data. Available from http://ndas.cwla.org/NWG/WorkGrp/NWG_CMinFC_FinalCopy.PDF.

Holden, W., & Morton, T. (1999). *Designing a comprehensive approach to child safety. Child Welfare Institute and Action for Child Protection*. Atlanta, GA: National Resource Center on Child Maltreatment

McFadden, E. J., & Ryan, P. (1991). Maltreatment in family foster homes: Dynamics and dimensions. In M. Robin (Ed.), *Assessing child maltreatment reports* (pp. 209–232). Binghamton, NY: Haworth Press.

National Clearinghouse on Child Abuse and Neglect. (2000). *Child abuse and neglect state statutes elements: Investigation: Number 15. Authorization for multidisciplinary team*. Available from http://www.calib.com/nccanch/pubs/stats00/mdt.pdf.

National Resource Center on Child Maltreatment. (2000). *Safety assessment and planning: An overview* (Handout packet for technical assistance meeting at Massachusetts Department of Social Service). Boston, MA: Author.

Office of Juvenile Justice and Delinquency Prevention. (2000). *Portable guides to investigating child abuse: Forming a multidisciplinary team to investigate child abuse*. Available from http://www.ojjdp.ncjrs.org/resources.

Rycus, J., & Hughes, R. (1998). *Field guide to child welfare*. Washington, DC: Child Welfare League of America.

Schene, P. (2001). *Meeting each family's needs: Using differential response in reports of child abuse and neglect*. The National Resource Center for Family Centered Practice. Available from www.cwresource.org/aboutus.htm.

Sheppard, D., & Zangrillo, P. (1996). Coordinating investigations of child abuse: Guidelines for collaboration between law enforcement agencies and child protection agencies. *Public Welfare, 54*, 21.

Tjaden, P. G., & Anhalt, J. (1994). The impact of law enforcement–child protective services investigations in child maltreatment cases. Denver, CO: Center for Policy Research.

Additional Resources

Casey Family Programs. (2001, December 3). *Child safety—Curricula for staff and families*. Available from http://www.casey.org/cnc/documents/child_safety_curricula_for_staff_and_foster_parents.pdf.

Child Welfare League of America. (2002). *NWG highlights—Child maltreatment in foster care: Understanding the data*. Washington, DC: CWLA National Working Group to Improve Child Welfare Data. Available from http://ndas.cwla.org/NWG/WorkGrp/NWG_CMinFC_FinalCopy.PDF.

Child Welfare League of America. (2002). *NWG highlights—Placement stability measure and diverse out of home populations*. Washington, DC: CWLA National Working Group to Improve Child Welfare Data. Available from http://ndas.cwla.org/NWG/WorkGrp/NWG_PlcmtChanges040502.pdf.

Freeman, L. (2002) *National Foster Parent Association allegation resource manual*. Gig Harbor, WA: National Foster Parent Association. Information available from http://nfpainc.org.

Greenblatt, S., & Lutz, L. (2000). *Dual licensure of foster and adoptive parents: Evolving best practice*. Seattle, WA: Casey Family Programs.

Iowa Foster and Adoptive Parents Association. (1999) *The child abuse assessment: A guide for foster parents*. Ankeny, IA: Author. Available from http://www.ifapa.com/Brochures/ca_assessment.pdf.

National Center for Resource Family Support, Casey Family Programs. (n.d.). *Inventory of respite resources*. Available from http://www.casey.org/cnc/support_retention/respite_inventory.htm.

National Resource Center on Child Maltreatment. (2003, March). *Maltreatment in out-of home placement: A leadership initiative of the National Resource Center on Child Maltreatment*. Atlanta, GA: Author. Available from http://www.gocwi.org/nrccm/.

Office of the Inspector General, U. S. Department of Health and Human Services. (2002, May). *Recruiting foster parents* (OEI-07-00-00600). Washington, DC: Author. Available from http://oig.hhs.gov/oei/reports/oei-07-00-00600.pdf.

Office of the Inspector General, U. S. Department of Health and Human Services. (2002, May). *Retaining foster parents* (OEI-07-00-00601). Washington, DC: Author. Available from http://oig.hhs.gov/oei/reports/oei-07-00-00601.pdf.

Expert Panel and Reviewers*

Jenifer Agosti, Research Analyst, Casey National Center for Resource Family Support, Casey Family Program, N. Andover, MA

Kathy Barbell, Director, Casey National Center for Resource Family Support, Casey Family Program, Washington, DC

Patsy L. Buida, MSW, Foster Care Specialist, Children's Bureau, U.S. Department of Health and Human Services, Washington, DC

Jesslyn Cobb, Program Specialist III, Child Protective Services Program, Virginia Department of Social Services, Richmond, VA

Janice Ereth, PhD, Director, Children's Research Center, National Council on Crime and Delinquency, Madison, WI

Stephen Este, Operational Analyst, Texas Department of Protective and Regulatory Services, Austin, TX

Jean Fiorito, Executive Director, Connecticut Foster Parent Association, Rocky Hill, CT

Trish Foster, Director of Quality Management, Casey Family Program Headquarters, Seattle, WA

Lana Freeman, Tarrant County Foster Parent Association President, National Foster Parents Association Region VI Vice President, Foster Parent Issues and Allegation/ Chair, Kennedale, TX

Sondra Jackson, Executive Director, Black Administrators in Child Welfare, Washington, DC

Pauline Koch, Executive Director, National Association for Regulatory Administration, Dover, DE

Gary Mallon, DSW, Center Director, National Resource Center for Foster Care and Permanency Planning, Hunter College School of Social Work, City University of New York, New York, NY

Janet K. Motz, MSW, Child Protection Program Administrator, Child Welfare Services, Colorado Department of Human Services, Denver, CO

Catherine M. Nolan, MSW, Director, Office on Child Abuse and Neglect, Children's Bureau, U.S. Department of Health and Human Services, Washington, DC

---

* Affiliations as of November 2001.

Michael Nunno, DSW, Family Life Development Center, NYS College of Human Ecology, Cornell University, Ithaca, NY

Cathy Roark, Assistant Director of, Practice and Policy Development, Casey Family Program Headquarters, Seattle, WA

Betsy Rosenbaum, Director of Children and Family Services, American Public Human Services Association, Washington, DC

Barry Salovitz, Director, National Resource Center on Child Maltreatment. Glenmont, NY

Rhonda Smith, Licensing Supervisor, Chicago Commons, Chicago, IL

Lynhon Stout, Executive Director, Iowa Foster Parent Association, Ankeny, IA

Jake Terpstra, Retired, Grand Rapids, MI

Rose Washington, Executive Director, Berkshire Farm Center and Services for Youth, Cannan, NY

The following individuals served solely as reviewers:

Theresa Costello, MA, Deputy Director, ACTION for Child Protection, Inc. and National Resource Center on Child Maltreatment, Albuquerque, NM

Karen Jorgenson, Administrator, National Foster Parent Association, Gig Harbor, WA

Robert Lindecamp, Senior Policy Associate, American Public Human Services Association, Washington, DC

Pam Pearson, Oregon Department of Human Services, Children, Families and Adult Group, Salem, OR

Peter Pecora, Manager of Research Services, Casey Family Programs, and Professor, School of Social Work, University of Washington, Seattle, WA

Authors and CWLA Staff

Authors

Gary Calhoun, PhD, Assistant Professor of Social Work, Bridgewater State College, Bridgewater, MA

Caren Kaplan, ACSW, Program Manager for Child Protection, Child Welfare League of America, Washington, DC

Millicent Williams, ACSW, Director of Foster Care, Child Welfare League of America, Washington, DC

CWLA Contributing Staff

Lloyd Bullard, Director of Residential Group Care

Pam Day, Director of Child Welfare Services and Standards

Betty Johnson, Senior Consultant

John R. George, Senior Consultant

Maureen Leighton, Director of Training

Linda Jewell Morgan, Director of National Projects

Mattie Satterfield, Director of Kinship Care

Linda Spears, Acting Associate Vice President, Communications and Corporate and Individual Giving

Ada White, Director of Adoption

Kristen Woodruff, Project Manager, National Working Group to Improve Child Welfare Data